such were some of you

such were some of you

The Spiritual Odyssey of an Ex-Gay Christian

Kevin Linehan

HERALD PRESS
Scottdale, Pennsylvania
Kitchener, Ontario
1979

Library of Congress Cataloging in Publication Data

Linehan, Kevin, 1948-
  Such were some of you.

    1. Linehan, Kevin, 1948-   2. Christian biography
—United States. 3. Homosexuals—United States—
Biography. 4. Homosexuality and Christianity.
I.   Title.
BR1725.L446A35   248'.2 [B]   79-12178
ISBN 0-8361-1890-1

SUCH WERE SOME OF YOU
Copyright © 1979 by Herald Press, Scottdale, Pa. 15683
    Published simultaneously in Canada by Herald Press,
    Kitchener, Ont. N2G 4M5
Library of Congress Catalog Card Number: 79-12178
International Standard Book Number: 0-8361-1890-1
Printed in the United States of America
Design: Alice B. Shetler
Cover photo: H. Armstrong Roberts

15 14 13 12 11 10 9 8 7 6 5 4 3 2 1

This book is affectionately dedicated to
John Squires and **Beverly Blades,** my
father and mother in the Lord, in the spirit
of 1 Corinthians 4:15. Were I the only
Christian they ever discipled, their reward in
heaven would be abundant and overflowing.

Contents

Introduction

It takes years for some friendships to develop. Other friendships emerge in a short period of time. The development of my friendship with Kevin Linehan was the latter.

My wife and I, with one of our daughters, visited Kevin in Reno, Nevada, on July 7, 1977. Our evening together was most delightful. He shared with us his spiritual pilgrimage of deliverance from living a gay life to living for Jesus Christ. Our hearts were thrilled and warmed by the testimony.

The problem of homosexuality is a live issue today— one that is filled with deep emotion. It is an issue in politics, in education, in business, and in the church. No part of our society remains unaffected.

Many voices, often conflicting, are being heard. Some people are speaking out because they feel threatened by homosexuals; some are speaking out because they feel God is calling them to expose gays; others are speaking because they have studied the problem. Persons living the gay life are openly defending it, and other persons who have been delivered from living the gay life are telling of their new-found life. All feel deeply about their opinions and their convictions.

Such Were Some of You, is important to the Christian church because it is the firsthand account of a person who found the gay life empty and unfulfilling, and who found deliverance from living that life-style through Jesus Christ.

I consider *Such Were Some of You* a valuable contribution to the dialogue on homosexuality. Hopefully, persons who are disillusioned with their gay life will also find deliverance through Jesus Christ.

                          Lloyd Weaver, Jr.
                          Newport News, Virginia

                          March 21, 1979

Author's Preface

The Apostle Paul, writing in 1 Corinthians 6:9-11, stated that he knew of believers in the church at Corinth, over which he exercised apostolic authority, who had been redeemed from lives of homosexual sin through the acceptance of Jesus Christ as personal Lord and Savior. He did not speak of this fact in a whisper, fearful of arousing the sensitivities of Christians too timid to hear such things discussed in public. Nor did he proclaim this fact with apprehension about how it would be received by pharisaical disciples, still too carnal to accept such converts into full fellowship and office in their assembly. Rather, God's chosen apostle to the Corinthian church, his evangelist to the Gentiles, declared with open praise and rejoicing that the gospel message had borne fruit in the lives of some we, today, would call "gay."

His Lord Jesus had extended a gracious invitation to salvation from the guilt of sin, freedom from its power, and ultimate deliverance from its very presence, to "whoever believes in him" (John 3:16). The spirit of this invitation was clear when Christ told Nicodemus, "I did not come into the world to condemn the world, but that the world might be saved through me" (John 3:17, paraphrased).

In announcing the fact that this good news had been received, even by those who had previously been involved in a lifestyle of homosexual sin, Paul was bearing testimony to the fulfillment of Christ's proclaimed provision. And that's what I am attempting to do, as well, in this book.

I do not claim to speak for all gays when I describe my thoughts and feelings prior to accepting Jesus, any more than I claim to speak for all ex-gays (or Christians per se for that matter) when I describe my experiences after finding Christ. I have met many homosexuals and ex-homosexuals whose lives have been much different from my own. In baring my soul in this book, my primary purpose is to proclaim what God has done in this once-gay Christian's heart. I know now that if our heavenly Father liberated a soul as desperately depraved as I, He can and will work His miracles in whoever comes to Him for salvation and deliverance.

The various negative encounters I recall with some evangelicals (of both Pentecostal and non-Pentecostal persuasions) have not been glossed over. They are true and must be included to keep the book honest and straightforward as an autobiographical work. In discussing these experiences, I in no way mean to imply a spirit of condemnation toward any individual or group. Rather, I hope the truths found in these incidents will exhort and encourage Christian churches suffering similar problems. Perhaps retelling my experiences will help them realize the impact such doctrines or practices can have on the lives of new believers, whether these "babes in Christ" come from gay backgrounds or not. Such a spirit is biblical. I sincerely hope that the fruit of this exhortation may yet yield much benefit in the lives of those still to be born into God's kingdom.

A brief explanation of my use of the term "ex-gay" may be in order here. Many Christians object to this term, since everyone in the body of Christ is an ex-something. I heartily agree. Moishe Rosen faces a similar problem. He frequently uses the term "Jews for Jesus," although we are told that there is neither Jew nor Gentile in Christ. However, I agree with Rosen and other movements which employ such terminology as an aid to effective communication. The terms ex-gay, Jews for Jesus, or whatever, are simply rhetorical devices which necessity demands in certain ministries.

Unfortunately, many members of the Universal Fellowship of Metropolitan Community Churches who profess to be Christians and yet have not given up their homosexual practices surround us. They refer to themselves as Christians, or sometimes as gay Christians. In ex-gay ministry, it is easy to become involved in some devastating experiences which result from improper terminology, unless one is able to employ some means of effectively conveying scriptural concepts. Thus I have chosen to use the term ex-gay throughout this book to identify the Christian who has forsaken his gay lifestyle and practices, as opposed to the professing Christian who has not.

Finally, let me comment on some preconceptions or apprehensions with which the reader may approach this work. According to the views expressed in the gay community, only about 10 percent of practicing homosexuals frequent gay bars. The stereotyped view of homosexuals as effeminate drag queens (men dressed in woman's clothing) is inaccurate. Fully 90 percent of the 10 to 12 percent of our population which is homosexual are closet gays. They are homosexuals who live next door, go to the office daily, are married with one or more children, and are never associated with the gay community in any way. In fact they hide their homosexuality with a tenacity that is borne out of dread and anxiety of "blowing their cover" and being discovered. Oh, what desperate lives they lead! How good it would be for them to have someone, anyone, whom they could trust, and with whom they could discuss their quiet lives of loneliness!

That's the kind of homosexual I once was. It is primarily to such persons that this book will appeal, and it is generally this type of gay that the Christian encounters in his ministry. Anyone reading this book with the idea that it will reveal a life of total homosexual abandon, sensationalizing the sexual exploits of a person seeking nothing more in life than erotic pleasure, will be sorely disappointed. Gays are people just as truly as those who do not engage in sinful sex acts of a homosexual nature. Their lives are rich with the experience of all aspects of their personhood, including the emotional, physical, spiritual, intellectual, and social. Sex as an expression of one's sexuality is an important component of most people's humanity, yet it is not the primary focal point of most people's lives whether they are gay or straight.

Many brothers and sisters who have never engaged in homosexual sin, yet have been involved in premarital sexual encounters or extramarital affairs, would be shocked—and justifiably so—to see a book which purports to portray a non-gay's life focused primarily around such sexual episodes. Such a book could not be written by an average non-gay man. It could only be written by a person with sexual compulsions abnormal to either the homosexual or the heterosexual lifestyles per se.

This book, then, will not take you into the gay bars or baths for a look at supposedly normal homosexual orgies. Rather, it describes the life of one homosexual, now a Christian, who lived where most homosexuals live—in the farm communities, towns, suburbs, cities, high schools, colleges, hospitals, military bases, prisons, and, yes even churches, of our post-Christian society.

Surrounded by constant references to homosexuality in the mass media, and by homosexual practices among family, friends, neighbors, employees, fellow students— even professing Christians—a testimony of healing and deliverance may be in order. Don't you agree?

It would be virtually impossible to thank all the people who have made this book possible. Yet, it would also be thoughtless not to thank some of them.

My father and mother deserve the greatest mention here. The Linehans tried to tell me for a long time that I had a talent for writing, and as with so many other things, I did not listen to them when I should have. Yet their encouragement was paramount in finally obtaining the courage I needed to try my first book.

Henry Chappell and Jeff Taylor labored over the typing of the manuscript for hours and days. Without their concern, many more all-night sessions would have been required to complete it.

Betty Squires offered a hug in the Spirit, a compassionate heart, and a ready ear when I became discouraged. Without this precious sister's help, I might have succumbed to depression and frustration, perhaps never completing the work at all.

Ten individuals and/or families reviewed a draft of the manuscript, offering helpful exhortation and advice. Without their encouragement my trembling heart would often have fainted. They deserve and have my deepest gratitude.

My experience has shown me that it is only out of deep involvement in communal living that knowledge is transformed into wisdom, and that ability to fruitfully convey one's life for Jesus and the lost is received. The brothers at the house ministry where I reside have constantly affirmed me in a manner that I never believed was possible on earth. The affirmation of these fellow Christians is one of the greatest gifts the Lord has ever given me and I pray that their support will bear ample fruit in this book.

My house church group (originally called the Reno Mennonite Fellowship and now known as the Risen Saviour's Christian Fellowship) is a testimony of God's healing, cleansing, and strengthening love. Without acceptance by this community I would have despaired of learning to live a Christian life pleasing to God at all. Through the effectual working of each of its individual parts, the Lord has caused my growth. Even at the cost of the time involved, this church has provem its love for gays and ex-gays everywhere by freeing me to the task of sharing my testimony with them here. Without their permission and patience this book would have remained only a dream.

From the first Mennonite I ever met, to the publishers of this book, I have witnessed a courage and conviction, a love and affirmation, which bespeaks a total willingness to reach out to gays and ex-gay Christians the world over.

Paul M. Schrock, my editor, and Herald Press, my publishers, are living witnesses that Jesus stands with outstretched hands to everyone in need, offering them acceptance, assistance, and encouragement. Without these brothers, untold numbers of those who are now such as I once was would remain without this testimony.

Kevin Linehan, Minister
The Risen Saviour's Christian Fellowship
P.O. Box 8348
Reno, Nevada 89507

Homosexual Hotline Number
(702) 786-9352

such were
some of
you

In keeping silent about evil, in burying it deep within us, so that it appears nowhere on the surface, we are implanting it, and it will rise up a thousandfold in the future.

—Alexander Solzhenitsyn in
The Gulag Archipelago

1
A Basket on the Nile

The Jochebed Fantasy

There seems to be a bit of Job in every person. Each of us cries out for answers to the burning questions of our hearts at one time or another. I will never forget the night God revealed for me the why's and wherefore's of my past. Through a spiritual encounter with Him, I was freed to praise Him in a deeper dimension than I ever could before. From that time on, I have also been able to accept the experiences of my early childhood in a manner I never dreamed was possible. Truly, it was a compassionate confrontation.

I was alone that eventful evening, reading the biblical account of Jochebed and Moses. Trying to picture everything carefully in my mind, I saw Jochebed drawing forth all the courage of her soul, while picking her way delicately through lush green reeds along the muddy Nile River. Tall and shapely, with large almond-colored eyes and raven hair, she was easily recognizable as the mother of the beautiful three-month-old baby boy clutched so tightly at her breast.

Searching for a solid place to stand in the shallow water, she quickly glanced over her right shoulder. No, none of the slaves navigating three reed boats, which meandered slowly down the river under an intensely hot desert sun, had seen her on the bank. Neither had they heard the water splash as she gingerly placed the little child inside the black, tar-covered basket, floating at her knees.

Then, just for a moment, Jochebed's will failed her. Like a magnet touching iron, her hands absolutely refused to pull away from the scarlet covers arranged so carefully around her son. She prayed with all the fervor of a mother's heart, now enflamed by the sad and frightening situation: "Jehovah, if I did not know that Pharaoh would kill my child, were I to keep him, I would never give him up—no, not for any reason! Give me strength to do that which I must do to save his life. Shelter him under the shadow of Your wings. Bless him and give him all that You alone, from this moment on, can give him. Make him great and holy in Your sight."

With a last tear falling from the corner of her eye upon the scarlet blanket, she tore her hands away, giving the ark a determined push out into the gentle current. Then, turning swiftly, she rushed from the bank with a final stolen stare at the now rapidly disappearing basket, fading slowly into the shadows of the tall palm trees which lined the narrow road not far from shore.

Just as Jochebed became immersed in the shadows, the entire picture vanished from my mind. Tears were coming to my eyes. I focused my attention on three compelling aspects of the narrative. First, I noted Jochebed's love for her infant son. Then I realized she had been compelled to leave little Moses on the Nile by forces over which she had absolutely no control. And, finally, I recognized this Jewish mother's faith, placed securely in her God, who alone could be trusted with her precious floating treasure.

For some unexplained reason, these factors of the story hurt me deeply. Soon questions began to pound away at my consciousness demanding answers I simply could not give. Reading the story had brought to mind all the submerged pain inherent in facing a past which had left me scarred and filled with unresolved frustration.

Why had I been abandoned at birth without the mother's love which Moses knew? Why couldn't I believe that somewhere, even at the moment of our fateful final parting, a similar love to that which Jochebed possessed had burned brightly in the deep recesses of my own real mother's heart? Why had she abdicated her throne of motherhood? Her will had not been forced: she had simply chosen to leave me. These questions compelled me to search my memory, focusing attention on the few barren facts recorded about my birth.

Unresolved Memories

It had been a cold, perhaps even snowy day, that March 23 thirty years ago when I was born. The only thing certain about my birth (aside from its place and date) still known to me was that, at the moment it occurred, my mother found herself with her second unwanted and fatherless child. My half brother, Chip, had arrived only fourteen months before!

I did not know whether Mother ever held me in her arms or not. If so, those caresses at her breast were not to

change her predetermined plans. Before the first daf-
fodils had poked their stems through the newly thawed
ground of that year's springtime, both my brother and I
had already been abandoned to the care of the New York
State Department of Social Services.

Six sterile years followed this abandonment. I never
knew whether we had three sets of foster parents, or
twice that number. None had touched me deeply in any
special loving way. Their faces were all lost in a labyrinth
of yesterdays. Their actions, however, I could not forget.

At age three, I was locked in a car several hours. Barely
able to see through the ice and snow covering its windows, I almost froze. Still in pajamas, during the early
hours of the morning, I had neither hat nor coat. The
heater was off. No one responded to my cries. My foster
parents had responded to my crying earlier. The car was
their response!

Some months later, perhaps in another home (I
couldn't quite recall), a quick stab with a fork by my
"father" taught me not to reach across a dinner table. No
scar remains on my fingers from this encounter. Only my
heart was wounded.

I learned the difference between some foster parents
and a real mother when I crushed a light bulb in my
hand one afternoon. Running to my "mother," bleeding
all the way, I heard her scream, "Get out, get out, you're
bleeding all over my freshly washed kitchen floor!"

Spinning quickly on my heels to avoid this new and
somehow deeper pain, I ran off once again, this time into
the woods bordering our property, desperately seeking
solitude in which to nurse my throbbing hand. Pulling
the pieces of shattered glass from the skin wasn't easy. A
long jagged scar remains to this day. I wondered mostly,

however, about the pain in my heart. It seemed worse than my cut hand, a wound that might never heal.

At age five, fear paralyzed me again. This time I was informed in a loud voice that I would be locked in a dirty chicken coop all night for melting crayons on a small humidifier near our beds. Only after accompanying my "father" down the hall some distance, kicking and screaming in terror, was I allowed to return to the bedroom with the punishment unfulfilled.

Up to this point in my life, no one had ever taught me about God. Yet somehow an intuitive knowledge of Him must have been present deep within my soul at birth. I can't remember a time when at least the thought of God was unknown to me. As I returned to our room that horrible night, barely escaping the chicken coop discipline, I prayed my first prayer. Equating death with old age in my young mind I begged, "Lord, please let the next 'parents' we have be old so they will die soon."

Trying to sleep, visions of huge chickens clawing and pecking me to death precluded any rest. I begged my brother once again for the permission he sometimes gave when nightmares came. He answered, "Yes." Curling myself up in a little ball by tucking my knees up to my chin, thus taking as little room at the foot of his bed as possible, I promptly fell asleep, secure at last in the presence of the one stable person in my ever changing world, my brother, Chip. Oh, how I loved him!

A Dark Night of my Soul

Recalling these experiences of my early childhood, after reading from Exodus, had resolved nothing. Thinking about the love Moses had known while at his mother's breast, only served to make my pain worse. I was filled with questions, but answers wouldn't come. I knew I did not have them in me. I didn't feel anyone could give them to me. Yet, I couldn't live without them.

In the same manner that Jochebed had done so many hundreds, even thousands of years before me, I turned to God, pouring out all my questions at His throne. I felt that no one but He alone could stop my burning tears, forever resolving the debilitating frustration deep within my soul. As I picked up my Bible, hoping for answers I knew must come from its pages, fear suddenly gripped me. This was no ordinary situation! Anxiety encapsulated itself in a chilling thought. What if God did not respond? I couldn't live another hour with these questions tearing my heart apart. I rememberd a song I had heard some time before. Singing it softly to myself brought the courage I needed to believe God would never let me down. Over and over I sang the words:

> Has He ever failed to see you through
>   in your darkest hour?
>
> Has the Savior ever failed to be a strong
>   and mighty power?
>
> Has He ever left you in your despair?
>
> When you called on Him, did you find Him there?
>
> Has He ever failed you one time? Has He ever
>   failed you yet?

Recalling that God had never failed me before armed me with a new and deeper faith. Opening my Bible again, I read verse after verse, then chapter after chapter, from the Old Testament as well as the New. Suddenly it happened! God began to respond. Three verses of Scripture stood out now. They appeared on the screen of my mind in gold letters on a black background. I knew they were just the ones the Holy Spirit had chosen to speak to my need at that particular moment.

I read the first one, Genesis 50:20. Here Joseph was speaking to his brothers who had sold him into slavery in Egypt many years before. Joseph said, "You meant evil against me, but God meant it for good." The application of this insight in my own life couldn't be denied. Although my mother had not meant to hurt me in the way Joseph's brothers had hurt him, her irresponsibility, her sinful life of fornication outside of marriage, climaxed by her abandoning me at birth had definitely worked to my evil. The abuse I suffered in foster placement paralleled this. Yet God used all her sin to my good. I knew this definitely from the second Scripture.

Almost shouting with joy I read Romans 8:28, "All things . . . work together FOR GOOD to those who love God, to those who are called according to His purpose." *All things,* I thought . . . *for good.* I laughed. . . . *ALL THINGS work together FOR GOOD . . . to those who love God, to those who are called according to His purpose.* That I was called according to His purpose I knew well from having been born again the year before. Nothing could dull the application. Even the painful experiences of lonely rejection I had endured were not to become ugly trophies left for Satan, destined to blur my vision of God's love. No, the God who cannot lie said He used even these for my good.

Finally, thrilled with this new discovery, I devoured Psalm 27:10 like dessert at a three-course meal. "For if my father and mother should abandon me, You would

welcome and comfort me." (*The Living Bible*). My soul
sang! Praise bubbled forth from somewhere so deep inside me I knew its source must be the Holy Spirit. God
had allowed every incident, every experience I was remembering, for my good. His Father's heart prompted a
call to me in line with His own purposes. These purposes
included raising me up and making me His own Son!

Tears of self-pity departed quickly. They vanished
amidst the softly prayed alleluias of my soul at peace.
Regaining my composure I recalled that God is sovereign
in His universe. He could have prevented each single incident of my childhood, or all of them. Yet He had not.
In the secret counsels of His own foreknowledge He
knew that He could reproduce within my heart something of His own character through these unpleasant circumstances. Because of my own hurts, I would become
ever open to the man crushed in loneliness, the woman
scarred in separation, and the adolescent pained in rejection. I would learn empathy and realize that mercy is
love in full bloom. Sensitivity to the needs of a broken
and suffering world would be the fruit produced in my
heart by the Lord through it all.

Postscript to the Experience

Exciting encounters with the Lord (and ourselves
before His throne) often cut even Bible study short. Thus
I closed the Scriptures that evening content with a new-
found ability to integrate my childhood into the plan of
God for my life. Later I was to read on, past the biblical
account I studied then, following Moses' life with deep
interest.

It seems that Miriam, Moses' sister, had watched from
the shore as Jochebed floated her son upon the waters.

She saw Pharaoh's barren daughter lift the little child out of the basket, claiming him for her own. Although Jochebed's prayers were answered by Jehovah, even to the point of her being allowed to nurse her son, God eventually gave Moses over to the care of another family.

My own life experiences remarkably paralleled Moses' even here. When I was six, Mrs. Shore, our kind social worker, took my brother and me for a visit to the Bronx Zoo. Such outings were rare. Seeing this black and beautiful woman always seemed to mean a change of homes for us.

At lunch as I spoke excitedly about the thrilling sights and smells experienced at the zoo and my brother Chip devoured everything edible in sight, we were unaware of two strangers at a nearby table. Like Miriam, they simply observed. Like Pharaoh's daughter, they had no children!

There was no way of knowing that Mr. and Mrs. Linehan would pluck the basket containing not one child, but two from the Nile of life at that time. Months would pass prior to our meeting them face-to-face and being introduced. It was a life-changing encounter. Soon afterward, Chip and I were no longer without a family. The Linehans had seen to that.

Our new parents never told us what had passed through their minds as they watched us at lunch that day unnoticed. They seem not to have cared that by this time we were listed officially as "unadoptable" on the state rolls because of our ages. I was six and Chip was seven. It had become practically impossible to find a home for us, as most couples wanted younger boys, unscarred by the traumatic experiences of foster placement from an early age. Perhaps we were also unlikely to be adopted because the state refused to let Chip and me be separated. Still, this didn't matter to the couple who had seen us some months before. They wanted to become our dad and mom from that day forward, and their wishes were to be fulfilled.

2

Surpassing My Kinsman?

Parents of His Choosing

Our new parents were middle-aged, middle-class intellectuals. Dad, as we soon learned to call him, was heavyset with dark black hair, blue eyes, red fleshy cheeks, muscular forearms, and large hands. Mom was slightly taller than I would have expected. She maintained a casual bearing and seemed externally shy, though at heart she was confident and secure. A common philosophy of life had cemented our parents marriage into a union which was well able to withstand the strains and pressures a quarter of a century and two foster children hurled its way.

Dad was in his forties when we were adopted. He was of Irish descent (a fact about which he was very proud and which drove him to march in the St. Patrick's Day Parade with the Hibernians down Fifth Avenue each March 17), and had grown up in Boston, Massachusetts. His loyalty to his country had been proven in the socially "acceptable" manner of service in the military during the Second World War. Attainment of the Bachelor of Science and Master of Science Degrees qualified him for the highly responsible position of Custom's Inspector on the ships at New York Harbor, where he was employed by the United States Deparament of Agriculture. He worked long days, often putting in overtime, and commuted to his job hours before the rest of us even had to get up and ready ourselves for the day.

In many ways my father was a passive-dependent person easily manipulated, at least superficially, by my mother. I sensed this and disliked it intensely. Gentleness characterized his personality, however, unless he became irritated by something he could not avoid which threatened him. He was a peacemaker of the worldly kind, drawing his final conclusions philosophically from a heart filled with pragmatism.

Due in part to his heavy work schedule (although perhaps because my mother surpassed him in ability at such tasks as well), Dad seldom concerned himself with carpentry, painting, or other household repairs. He never drove the car, handled large sums of money, or disciplined us boys, except on rare occasions. When it came to administering physical punishment, fear probably had something to do with his reluctance to become involved. Dad was strong and he knew it. It was not really part of his nature to risk a confrontation with "the kids" which might have left us severely hurt, if he had forgotten himself. Thus, much of the role usually assigned to the husband in a marriage was left to Mom's considerable talents for practical performance. Indeed it would not be overstating the case to give her the credit for truly having raised us.

Mother was ten years younger than dad, and seemed fit for every task she ever assumed. She had been raised on a farm in Iowa, where an accident with a harrow left her father dead when she was only a child. Handling mature responsibility at a young age while assisting her mother in a store became her lot for some time. What drove her east when her mother died, I never knew. Yet, prior to this move at eighteen years of age, she had already taken her first degree, a Bachelor of Arts in Education at Northwest Missouri State Teacher's College. Later she obtained her Master of Arts and thirty-two credits beyond this from colleges in the East. Her name was mentioned as the able educator she was in both *Who's Who of American Women* and the *International Biography of Women,* prestigious publications whose demands for inclusion are very high. I never failed to marvel that her first class of high school students were older than she was at the time she taught them!

Yes, Mom was brilliant, eclectic concerning philosophy, and yet as basically pragmatic as my father. For all practical purposes, her will ultimately won out in all situations. Her energy was incredible. I never saw her watch television much, or read for any length of time for personal pleasure, because of the demands of being both a professional woman and a mother. She had few, if any, friends of the coffee klatch variety, and spent hours preparing lesson plans, doing housework, carpentry, and painting, attending the university, or assisting us boys with our homework, even after six long hours of teaching. If there ever was a personification of the work ethic it was Mother! I used to wonder if she was a workaholic driven by forces over which even she had little control.

There are some people who are more to be respected

than loved, more to be admired than related to on a deep level, more to be feared than enjoyed. Mom was a combination of all three. I respected her, admired her, and ultimately feared her. She was a woman you either agreed with, or were rejected by as ill, insolent, or ignorant. Nothing could salvage the self-esteem of anyone daring to confront her with a view differing from those she held sacred. Soft-spoken politeness always gave way to harshness under continued inquiry when I sought dialogue regarding differences of opinion. In the final analysis, Chip and I were to learn the cardinal rule that Dad had probably discovered many years before: "Mother is always right, and even if she isn't, she is anyway!" This I realized but being the damaged, insecure, overly verbal and strong-willed child I was, the battle lines were constantly drawn between Mom and me. Even Dad's reconciliatory nature could not keep him out of the crossfire. Time only deepened this problem.

Theologically, my parents represented a deceptive blend of orthodox Christian rhetoric that masked true spiritual ignorance. They believed that Jesus was God (so also was Allah, and the "god" of the Buddhists and Hindus). They accepted Christ's death on Calvary for them (as well as for all atheists, agnostics, and cultists of whatever variety). Faith was necessary to salvation (by this they meant faith in the "god" of any man's mind or culture). Holiness was essential for reception of divine approval (it was the type of goodness seen in the lives of Paul, Gandhi, Peter, and Muhammad). Heaven was received by an unconditional election (which occurred at death with some unknown basis apart from works).

Ultimately, "god" became lost in the practical daily experience of both Mother and Father's lives, as far as I could tell. The one absolute essential they did involve themselves with, however, was work—manifesting or proving their individual goodness or responsibility before the Lord. It was this "virtue" that they actually worshiped almost as an end in itself. To be good and to work hard were the chief goals of their lives. Yet, to me, this was never to become a sufficient integration point. Their spirituality was expressed in a sacramental system not unlike that of pre-Christian Judaism. Liturgical or formal prayer was made to Jesus in heaven, up there somewhere. It was hardly more than an enthusiastic appendage to an already conplete liberal Catholic lifestyle. I never heard either of my parents mention any prayer of theirs being answered. Material blessings and personal comfort did come, however, and were seen as the Lord's appropriate response to their hard labor on the job and in the home, combined with attainment of moral goodness in their lives per se.

Though both my parents accepted the concept of being "born again," this experience was equated with baptism (preferably at birth). Neither read the Bible, although Mom validated her personal faith with isolated "proof texts" lifted out of context, which she had memorized in a Congregational Sunday school as a child. Dad had no idea of what a personal encounter with Christ might entail. If such a thing were truly that important the priests would have informed him of it.

My latest parents considered evangelical Christianity valid (weren't all religions basically the same?) yet certainly a nuisance and more appealing to persons of lesser intellectual capability and formal academic achievement. They regarded themselves as people of sounder, broader religious persuasions than most evangelicals.

Premonastic Preparations: Six to Sixteen

The Linehans lived in a suburb of New York City, fifteen miles west of the George Washington Bridge, which connects northern New Jersey with Manhattan Island. Radburn, the section of Fairlawn in which their house was located, was a model community expertly designed by city planners during the 1930s to insure comfortable suburban living. All the streets except major thoroughfares were cul-de-sacs bordering lush green parks. Each park area boasted a large swimming pool, recreational facilities such as baseball fields, and a large two-story brick school. Few children had to cross even one street or walk more than fifteen minutes from their homes to reach their classes.

Thus not long after I joined the Linehan household in Fairlawn, I began a love affair with knowledge at the Radburn Elementary School. I was an excellent student from the first grade on. Reading and writing were talents that came as naturally to me as talking. They were received into my life with joy. Never did I find freedom from the almost mystic power over me that a good book possessed. I read everything capable of being understood by a child my age, even devouring some novels I never really comprehended at all.

Teachers throughout the first six grades appreciated intellectual ability wherever it could be discovered. They reinforced my thirst for knowledge with good grades and in every other way their own talents and abilities allowed.

Mom, being a teacher herself, encouraged academic interests by planning family vacations at historic sites across the entire Eastern Seaboard. By the time I reached junior high school age, we had visited The Gettysburg

Battlefield, Washington Monument, New York City Museum of Natural History and Planetarium, Liberty Bell, Bunker Hill, and Plymouth Rock, among many other places of historic interest. Each trip achieved at least one of Mom's desired effects: it always produced another question from Chip and me and illumined something new to arouse our curiosity.

Dad's interest in the physical sciences brought me as close to him as I was ever to become. He maintained a keen knowledge of biology and set up several aquariums in our home. I, too, developed an avid interest in tropical fish, eventually learning much about the delicate balance of the fresh-water tank. Dad seemed delighted that I had caught his interest. We spent many wonderful hours together at our hobby. Though not a lasting relationship, this brief invitation to friendship and intimacy with my father did much to motivate me toward attempting to understand his personality, which I had never admired. Our interest in tropical fish was something we could hold in common and share together beneath his carefully maintained superficial manner of relating to me.

Entering high school at fourteen, my attention became increasingly focused on religion. Each Sunday morning prior to mass, we attended Sunday school. Ever since first coming to live with the Linehans, Chip and I had been required to attend catechism class. Week after week, month after month, year after year, from first grade through ninth grade, we rarely missed a session. Thus we were deeply indoctrinated in Catholicism.

Entering Saint Catherine's Church, before we ever approached the classroom door, we could hear the unique, rhythmic, question-and-answer method of teaching employed by the Charity Nuns of Convent Station:

Question:	Who is God?
Answer:	God is an infinitely perfect Being who made all things and keeps them in existence.

Question:	Why did God make me?
Answer:	God made me to know Him, to love Him, and to serve Him in this world and to be happy with Him in heaven.

Question:	What is a sacrament?
Answer:	A sacrament is an external sign instituted by Christ to give grace.

On and on went the questioning session, drilling its teaching into the core of our minds. Few would ever forget what they were taught there, even if they never truly understood and integrated into their hearts anything of what they heard.

Because of my easily discernible ability of memorizing Catholic doctrine and my intense interest in spiritual things, I stood out above my fellow students in the eyes of our nun. Sister Mary Seton in her starched white wimple and long flowing veil and habit was revered almost as much as our priest. She began to take a personal interst in my religious development. Baptism at birth, communion at six, confirmation at twelve—these were a standard routine under the direct supervision of her religious order of sisters in much the same manner as puberty rites are administerd among pagan tribes in the jungles. Few participants of these sacraments developed much more than a nominal Catholicism, or spiritual interest, yet I did. "Young men like you," Sister Seton asserted, "might one day realize the highest life to which a young man in the Roman Catholic Church can aspire, the priesthood itself!"

No extended encouragement was actually needed from this nun to excite a desire for monastic living within my soul. Her interest in my spiritual development only paralleled my own. I had already accepted the belief that no greater pathway lay open to a sincere seeker after perfection than religious life in a monastery. Among men of similar spiritual zeal for their souls faults could truly be overcome, pride more easily erased, and sinful behavior patterns eradicated, or so I thought.

My parents readily affirmed a deep need within me for greater work on my faults and increased efforts after better living. However, they were noncommittal about my suggestion of seeking religious life in a monastery at the age of sixteen. Although they were staunch enough Catholics to send us to the nuns for religious education they did not share my enthusiasm for monasticism. Part of this was probably due to a sincere belief that living in a monastery under the vows of poverty, chastity, and obedience was not a normal life for most men. I discerned an added factor in their ambivalence, however. I think they misunderstood my true motives, attributing my desire to become "religious" as a form of self-exaltation, a wish to be numbered among the prophets when in their eyes my innate evilness proved I was more truly a wolf seeking sheep's clothing in assuming the monk's robe.

In fact, I was not planning to enter the monastery for self-glorification. It was true that I felt stifled at this time by my constant verbal battles with mother. Skirmishes were growing more heated as I grew into adolescence. I was deeply hurt by this. Yet I could not relate to Mom nor continue much longer to live at home without relating to her. I was constantly attempting to suppress the angry feelings I felt concerning her authoritarian attitudes. No longer was I naive enough to integrate all of her thoughts and feelings into myself. The nest was becoming increasingly uncomfortable. Even if she was right about my lack of holiness, I needed to get away from her harsh demands for conformity to her opinions and find others who did not seem to be against me because of my sin but rather were with me against my sin.

It was my sincere conviction that I needed to find a place to develop spiritually with others concerned about similar things. Perhaps by doing this I, too, could achieve some degree of success in my efforts to please God in heaven by producing appropriate "godly goodness." I needed to know if this was possible. If it was, it seemed to me that it had to be accomplished amidst those who understood my dilemma, who would work with me patiently instructing me how the law (Ten Commandments) was to be lived while sinful passions still raged within, always ready to strike out in anger, exalt self, or deny God's will. Somewhere men knew how to please God. Somewhere they had learned the secret of an iron-willed discipline, a formula for holiness creating saints out of sinful stuff such as I found within myself.

I no longer needed Mother to tell me how bad I was. I realized this as a basic fact already. What was needed now, she couldn't give. How was I to relieve the guilt which haunted me as a result of my lying to her so often? How could I do penance for stealing a fellow's money while attending holy mass itself? Where would I learn what had made me set the sofa on fire while flipping matches as a child, sending even confident Mother on a mad dash down the stairs to beat the leaping flames with a soggy towel? Why did I anger so easily? What could account for my not being able to shake these feelings of hostility toward Mom and Dad, who had given me every material thing I now possessed, although as a child I had been abandoned at birth. Perhaps the monks could lead me toward missing explanations. God would not have given us the law if we could not live its demands, would He? There must be a way to do it!

I wrote to every Catholic religious order in the United States which maintained a juniorate, learning their names from the *Catholic Directory*. Mailing these letters, I decided to walk to the library. There I might be able to find more literature showing me just which religious order I should choose.

Finding my way to the religion section, I recalled that I must read only works which had the imprimatur or seal of the Roman Catholic bishop of the diocese in which they were published, guaranteeing their freedom from theological heresy. Several caught my attention. They were written by a Trappist monk named Thomas Merton. Glancing quickly through their pages, I was immediately struck by the following words from *The Seven Storey Mountain*, in which this priest described his first weekend visit to Our Lady of Gethsamani Monastery in Kentucky:

> How did I live through that next hour? It is a mystery to me. The silence, the solemnity, the dignity of these Masses and of the Church, and the overpowering atmosphere of prayers so fervent that they were almost tangible choked me with love and reverence that robbed me of the power to breathe. I could only get the air in gasps.
> O my God, with what might you sometimes choose to teach a man's soul Your immense lessons! Here, even through only ordinary channels, came to me graces that overwhelmed me like a tidal wave, truths that drowned me

with the force of their impact: and all through the plain normal means of the liturgy—but the liturgy used properly, and with reverence by souls inured to sacrifice.

What a thing Mass becomes, in hands hardened by grueling and sacrificial labor, in poverty and abjection and humiliation! See, see, said those lights, those shadows in all the chapels. See who God is! Realize what this Mass is! See Christ here, on the Cross. See His wounds, see His torn hands, see how the King of Glory is crowned with thorns! Do you know what Love is? Here is Love suffering these nails, these thorns, that scourge loaded with lead, smashed to pieces, bleeding to death because of your sins and bleeding to death because of people that will never know Him and never think of Him and will never remember His sacrifice. Learn from Him how to love God and how to love men! Learn of this Cross, this Love, how to give your life away to Him.

The eloquency of this liturgy was even more tremendous: and what it said was one simple cogent, tremendous truth: this Church the Court of the Queen of Heaven is the real capitol of the country in which we are living. This is the center of all the vitality that is in America. This is the cause and reason why the nation is holding together. These men, hidden in the anonymity of their choir and their white cowls are doing for their land what no army, no Congress, no President could ever do as such: they are winning it the grace and the protection and the friendship of God.

By the time I had completed these passages my heart was pounding in my chest. Merton's words contained all the ideals and aspiration I possessed but had never been able to conceptualize or articulate for myself. I wanted desperately to do something for God. I needed to win His favor not only for others but most of all for myself. If holy performance of the mass as a sacrifice, the reenactment of Calvary by good men, could win God's grace, I knew that this was what I must do. Oh, how I longed to experience the nearness of the Lord, to be somehow (perhaps mystically?) involved with Him. To have Him come down from "up there" wherever heaven was and be close to me right here on earth. If, as Merton had said, all His blessings were mediated to me through the sacraments and liturgy of the church I must become immersed and permeated with them. I must lose myself in them, that I might find God and become one with Him as that monk had done. Then I could not only overcome my own sinfulness, but I could teach others the way to win God's approval through such works in monastic life as well.

My heart sang. I would join the band of Christ's true disciples, the holy monks of the Roman Catholic Church. Though the priests and nuns had told me many were called but few were chosen to acceptance in the monastery, I had every hope that I would be. Then even my parents would one day be proud of me because they would see that I had surpassed my kinsmen in the persuit of God. I could realize as Merton did, the asceticism, self-discipline, fasting, prayer, solitude, and labor of the truly zealous religious man.

Thomas Merton's books became almost a steady reading obsession with me. I devoured *The Seeds of Contemplation, The Secular Journal, Bread in the Wilderness, The Sign of Jonas,* and others, especially *The Waters of Siloe,* which relates the history of the Trappist monks through the centuries. I idolized those friars in their white habits and black scapulars, even writing poems about Merton himself. I actually believed that such men alone knew the secret of living a real life with God. Though the Trappists did not maintain a monastery for those as young as I, I was content in the fact that all orders of the church seemed somewhat alike regarding the monastic ideals they personified. Thus I was judged ready, willing, and qualified to join the Marist Order in their High School Preparation Seminary three months later in the fall of my junior year.

The Monastic Life: My Junior Year

The Marist Order was founded in France by Marcellin De Champagne to serve the Roman Catholic Church in the apostolate of teaching. Their schools dot the Eastern Seaboard of the United States and they were one of the few orders of brothers to prepare even high school students for their way of life prior to the Second Vatican Council. Not considered a truly monastic order, like the Trappists I had come to admire, they still lived the vows of poverty, chastity, and obedience in monasteries called brothers' residences. Their primary involvement was in the field of education. I was to enter their monastery which was located at that time on a mountaintop overlooking a beautiful lake outside the small town of Cold Spring, New York.

Driving up to the complex of buildings which resembled a medieval manor complete with a round turret, my first impression of the monks themselves was that they all seemed somehow similarly holy. This "holiness" appeared to be exuded not so much by their eyes being cast toward heaven, as by the long black robes and white rabats (rectangular starched collars) they wore and the four-inch crucifixes which dangled from their necks. There was something almost mystical about the monks which I couldn't explain.

Suddenly, we were at the entrance of the complex. Mom stopped the car and I swallowed hard, trying not to let her see the feeling of nervousness which had come over me. Before any last-minute changes of mind about returning home could take firm root in my consciousness, a tall, seventeen-year-old fellow student flashed a broad grin at me through the car window and reached for the door handle. My anxiety subsided. Hopping out of the car I shook his hand firmly. John was to become a lifelong friend. For the next two weeks he helped me adjust to the new and somehow slightly frightening world I had chosen to enter. He assisted me with a joy and kindness that caused me to admire, as well as respect him, almost immediately.

Entering the building, we arrived at a large dormitory. Row after row of beds and chests lined this hall-like room. The bed and chest assigned to me were to be, along with my schoolbooks, the only private possessions I used. Our white shirts, black pants, and black coats were all hung in a common closet off to one side of the dorm.

Divested now of the few pieces of luggage we had been carrying, John and I began our tour of the rest of the main monastery complex. My first impression of the chapel, dining room, classrooms, and locker rooms, with their row upon row of identical chairs, eating utensils, desks, and showers, convinced me quickly that individuality was soon going to become a dirty word. I was not mistaken.

Meeting with us in the chapel, which seemed to add a special solemnity to his words, Brother Dennis, our Superior, went to great lengths to explain to us the precise meaning of our being at the monastery. We were here to become *Marist Brothers!* This implied fitting into a certain Marist mold, and living a Marist lifestyle, forgetting about anything that would keep us from realizing the Marist ideals of superior academic achievement and religious zeal for the rules and regulations of the Marist order. Should we accomplish this to his satisfaction, we would be allowed to enter the next step of our training which would be undertaken after our graduation from high school. It consisted of two more years of learning about the Marist community in the United States and worldwide.

My heart sank. My desire was to be a monk like Thomas Merton and to learn how to live the law. Only now did I begin to see the distinctions between the very active religious orders and the contemplative ones. The meditative life Merton had described in his books, and for which I really longed, was giving way before my eyes to the academic competitive life of the Marists. This dilemma drove me to consider whether I should leave or stay! I realized there would be little personal relationship here. The brothers were probably able teachers and administrators, yet I saw little in them that led me to hope for love and understanding. I was never going to learn how to live the law by merely being given more laws to follow.

Finally, after this battle had raged within me some time, I decided to give it a few weeks. I would stay. Perhaps the Marist life had some hidden redeeming qualities somewhere yet to be discovered. Having come this far, I couldn't turn back now without giving it a chance. Were I to do so, I recognized that I would have to face much the same situation at home with Mother.

Perhaps I could learn something from the brothers which would assist me to understand myself and my world. Here, at least, I had the daily mass and sacraments with the liturgy, through which I believed the grace of God was mediated. In drawing close to Christ by

receiving His grace at the sacraments, I might just make
it yet.

My second day in the monastic life was filled with sur-
prises. Perhaps the most startling of these was to be
awakened at six o'clock in the morning by the click of the
light switch on the wall. Immediately, all sixty of us
dropped out of bed to our knees, under the somewhat
austere direction of Brother Perfect. After a short time of
group ritual prayer, we were allowed to dress and wash at
the basins in the washroom. Finding our way to the
chapel, somehow, in that semiconscious state I had always maintained prior to a good cup of tea after rising,
we all knelt on the kneelers at our pews. Confessions
were heard every day prior to mass. I was afraid to risk it
so soon. The priest, clad in a brown habit and sandals,
was a Capuchin monk, one of the strictest orders of the
Franciscan family. I wouldn't earn his wrath by admitting my sins of yesterday just yet.

Once the sacrament of penance was over, the mass
began. It was all in Latin, but we understood the general
idea of what was going on through having been raised
with the mumbled overtones of this foreign tongue since
we had first accompanied our parents to church many
years before. During this ritual, Merton's words came to
mind once again. This time, however, they held none of
the feeling I had associated with them earlier. Perhaps
tomorrow would bring a greater sense of Christ being
truly and physically present in the bread and wine.

Filing out of the chapel, two by two, we were allowed
to walk to the dining room. Here I began to learn the
strange manners of the monastic refectory. Standing by
our places at table, we maintained complete silence.
Brother Master, with Brother Perfect, marched to the

raised platform on which their separate table rested. Prayers began followed by the reading of a portion from Thomas A. Kempis' *Imitation of Christ*. Finally we were allowed to be seated. Would the little silver bell on the master's table be rung? If it was, we could talk to one another during the meal; if not, we were to eat in silence. Brother Dennis began to eat without touching the bell at all. Suddenly everyone was gesturing in monastic sign language. A shake of the wrist indicated Joe wanted some milk. A motion of the forearm brought the toast. Each of the students who served the tables understood this form of communication perfectly. Those of us who did not, tried as best we could, closely watching the others until we too understood each sign we saw.

My turn at dishes gave me new insights into institutional pot washing. Then, after helping mop the refectory floor, I had a few minutes left over to scurry off to the classroom and prepare myself for the first lesson of the day. I was terribly lonely in this new and strange environment, and unable to share my feelings with another soul. I prayed to Jesus, saying softly, "All for You, sweet Jesus, all for You, because I love You." Offering one's suffering to the Lord was considered a very holy thing to do. It might even bring special graces from God. Finally, shrugging off my loneliness as best I could, I opened my textbook just as Brother Patrick emerged through the door.

The subject of our first class was Mariology. We learned all the doctrine concerning Mary which the Catholic Church has developed through the centuries. Indeed the Lord's Mother was said to have remained a Virgin her entire life. She had been born without original sin and had been miraculously "assumed" into heaven.

By virtue of her holy life, she was invoked by the brothers in the order as their special patron saint. Prayers had a much better chance of being heard if we did not pray directly to God ourselves, but channeled our prayers through someone such as Mary whose holiness offered her a much better opportunity of gaining God's ear than we possessed ourselves.

Although none of this doctrine appears anywhere in the Scriptures, I never thought to question anything I was taught then. Bibles were certainly not required reading, and our list of articles to bring to the monastery never mentioned them. I had one or two Bibles at home and had read them occasionally, but not seriously enough to understand anything more than that Jesus was God and a great moral teacher who had died on the cross for the sins of everyone in the world.

Our texts for religious study never included the Scriptures. Instead, we studied the conjectures and opinions of the saints such as Thomas and Augustine, whose statements, along with those of the synods and councils of the church, were considered to be as authoritative as Scripture itself anyway. What teenager in our group would dared to have doubted a Bernard of Clairvaux or questioned an Ignatius of Loyola?

Secular study followed the teaching of church doctrine. My classes included English, chemistry, history, French, math, and typing. Throughout the day I came to understand more about these brothers who spent their lives teaching Catholic high school classes. Many of them were brilliant men, motivated by high ideals of religious living and academic pursuit. A few were neurotic or unstable, but most were normal, culturally bound Catholics, living a pre-Vatican II religious life which prided itself in their dedication and zeal. They could be counted on to teach children all they would ever need to know to become leaders of like faith in the church and larger social community.

As the last class of the day came to a close, we were informed that talking was permitted while recreation followed. Changing into our gym clothes we were assigned to play either football, soccer, or handball. My first love was handball (on a three-walled court with a hard Indian rubber ball), yet football was to be played as God's will for me that day. Doing the best I could to muster up some enthusiasm, I made a half-hearted attempt to show the other students I was not a complete loss to their team, but I don't think I was very convincing.

After recreation, we chanted the Divine Office, which consisted mostly of the Psalms. Unable to sing Gregorian or understand Latin yet, we were allowed to pray these prayers in English. It was during the reading of the Psalms that my spirit revived. Although I never understood exactly what they meant, and certainly had no idea of who had written them, these prayers somehow brought courage to my soul. I felt a kindred spirit with whomever their author might have been. He constantly seemed to be crying out to God for grace and mercy, both of which I needed desperatly myself. At the last "Amen," I reluctantly set the breviary in its place and headed for the dining room once again. After prayer we were allowed to speak to one another and this time as we ate I began to discover something about the other students.

Most of the young men who had found their way to this monastery were from Catholic homes and Catholic schools. To my knowledge, I was the only public school kid there. It became readily apparent to me that these young monks-to-be were the most outstanding students culled from the immense parochial school system of New York City. They were being groomed carefully to become the next generation of educators the Marist order would produce. All were intelligent (much more so than I) and they sincerely desired to serve God by devoting their lives to Him. Each took his vocation to religious life seriously, as did their parents, many of whom were extremely proud that their sons were to become some of the elite religious teachers of the church.

Friendships among the students were seriously discouraged. The fear of homosexual activity seemed to run high among the brothers on staff. I knew generally what I believed homosexuals to be but had never met a gay person myself. Certainly, I wasn't interested in such perverted behavior, yet the fear that it might occur somewhere in the monastery put a damper on all deep-felt conversations or relationships. Being alone or with one other student was always discouraged. Aside from our ordinarily highly organized existence, there was always at least one brother carefully watching the students at all times, even while we slept!

Out of all the brothers in the monastery, only John ever became my friend. But since he was a year older than I, we had little chance to spend much time together. Still, in the midst of a rather sterile and cold environment, his friendship was a treasured thing. I guarded it dearly. I needed at least one other student to whom I could turn in a time of crisis. John seemed able and willing to handle such a situation should it arise, and I had little doubt that he could.

After dinner and study hall came a brief period of recreation which was followed by more study. Homework was completed, themes were written, and formulas memorized. The day ended with a short conference led by Brother Dennis on a topic of his choice, followed by evening prayers. Only then would the lights be shut off in the dorm and Brother Perfect would walk up and down the rows of beds saying his rosary until we slept.

As time passed and the chilly winds of autumn signaled winter's approach, I found myself adjusting remarkably well to the monastic routine. Though I was never really the academic achiever I should have been in this highly competitive and scholarly environment, my deep desire to find holiness was a constant source of motivation to continue my training. I developed a deep affinity for the liturgy or ritual of the monastery. Merton had taught me, as well as the priests and brothers, that God's graces were always channeled through confession and communion. Thus, in spite of my sinfulness, I could count on the sacraments pulling me out of my emotional slumps.

The brothers assumed more friendly attitudes on occasion. Each was a unique character with a personality and set of mannerisms that differed from all the others in spite of the identical doctrine, clothing, rules, and lifestyle which they followed to the letter. Perhaps the brother for whom I had the most affection was Leo.

Brother Leo taught us math. He always appeared at class (the last one of the day) with a sweatsuit underneath his long monk's robe. He was as faithful and devout concerning his jogging as he was in his other religious exercises. Shortly after the bell for recreation rang, he would divest himself of his clerical garb, plop an ever present shower cap on his snow-white hair, and commence his jog into the hills of the surrounding landscape. This touch of individuality and personal involvement in a sport which made him happy (as unorthodox as he looked while pursuing it), won him a place in the hearts of most of his students.

One Saturday, while all of us were occupied in the unenviable task of cleaning out an old pigsty on the edge of the monastery grounds, Brother Leo rushed up to us with a loud shout. "The fire extinguishers," he yelled. "Quick, get the fire extinguishers from the main house and meet me by the hill leading to the lake! Hurry! Hurry! We must get the fire out before it reaches the teaching brothers' residence."

Seeing this kind old monk, who was usually so quiet and reserved (except during his jogging), shouting and gesturing toward the north, was enough to send all of us students running in various directions. John searched for the extinguishers from the main building, I dashed away to find those in the shower room, and Tom exploded into the classrooms calling for more help from the guys there.

Meeting together on the run toward the hillside, the story was shouted back and forth. Brother Leo had attempted to burn off some of the brush on the hill behind the brothers' residence. In doing so he had simply ripped up an old *New York Times* and threw burning pieces of it in various directions. Soon the wind had whipped the flames out of control and they were heading rapidly toward the residence. We had to put the fire out before the house was damaged.

Arriving at the fire we took a quick glance in the direction of the brothers' house. Much to our surprise, we saw Brother Gregory still seated with his back to the windows and us (as well as the flames) totally oblivious to the impending disaster, playing classical music on the grand piano. Although I should have worried for his safety, I fell to the ground in a spasm of laughter. As Brother Leo shouted, "To the right," to one crew of students with their extinguishers and then, "To the left," to another crew with their rakes, and Brother Gregory continued his concert, my mind conjured up images of Nero playing his fiddle while Rome burned! I just couldn't shake the thought. Gradually, when I had regained my composure and collected my thoughts, I joined in the mop-up work of beating out the final flames as they approached to within twenty feet of the brothers' residence.

Tiredly dragging ourselves back to the main monastery, covered by soot and ashes, with rakes and fire extinguishers in hand, we almost hugged Brother Leo. Although his carelessness could have caused severe damage to the monastery property, perhaps even injury to Brother Gregory, he had become our hero. He was imperfect. He had done something careless and stupid. He had sinned. He was human. He had failed. He was one of us. His informal hug of thanks and gratitude to us for helping him correct his error as best he could allowed the exterior facade of coldness and austerity the brothers always wore to shatter in a million pieces. In its place a mysterious and spontaneous group affirmation of love and compassion appeared at last. Seeing this feeling of warmth and acceptance mutually exchanged between monk and students convinced me that perhaps there was hope for finding my place among these men after all. Though it would probably be a slow process that could take years, the coals of love were there and who knew what winds of circumstance and shared experience might one day fan them into full flame.

It was during ice hockey season that I noticed a strange phenomenon taking place at breakfast. Brother Dennis rang the silver bell, allowing us to speak, less frequently than before. This led me to become more aware of things around me other than conversation. Day after day, there would be a vacant place at this table or that one. I knew what this meant. A chill of fear went through us all! Our class was dwindling rapidly. One after another of us was not measuring up to the expectations of the brothers. We were not assuming our identity as Marists in the accepted manner.

Brother Dennis's conferences became longer and longer prior to our retiring at night. The policy of monthly individual conferences was begun. Each of us was called into the brother's office individually for what he called "direction" and told that we were failing in given areas. We were to work harder, study more, pay better attention to Brother Prefect, and so on. But somehow this "direction" failed to stem the rising number of empty places at breakfast. In fact, the situation grew worse. I began to realize that my own fear of being asked to leave was a healthy sign that I had decided to remain forever in this order, to become the teaching brother I was "supposed" to become. Here, centering my attention on the sacraments, I was learning how to obey the law.

As the last day of the school year prior to summer vacation began, I was exuberant. I had made it! In spite of my poor grades, I had passed all my subjects. I could relax now. The Regents' examinations, three hours of testing in every subject area, including typing, was grueling, yet only a memory. Although only fifteen out of the original

sixty students still remained in my grade, and only
twenty were still present in the senior class (among
whom was my friend John), I had succeeded. I had not
been asked to leave.

For the first time since entering the monastery the
year before, I had come to believe in myself. I had been
accepted. I was a part of a group of people who, although
they did not emphasize personal relationships or even
contemplative monasticism, were concerned about living
a truly religious life. I did have to admit that I had not
learned much about how to become the good person I
wanted to be, but there was time for that. I was only in
high school. When I graduated the following year, I
could then go on to the novitiate, where the monks were
taught to worship God more and better through
increased periods of prayer and meditation. There I
would also show God the depth of my commitment
through taking the vows of poverty, chastity, and
obedience.

Holiness didn't happen overnight. My faults and sins
seemed no larger than those of my fellow students, many
of whom admitted to even deeper habits of sin than those
which I possessed. I needn't worry. My scale of relative
holiness didn't bother me much when I kept it geared to
the standard seen around me. God would reveal His
secrets of holiness one at a time through my superiors
and the monastic exercises and disciplines I would learn
in the years of training still to come.

Mom was driving up to the monastery this morning.
John and I had a wonderful talk and seemed to be growing deeper in our friendship. I would tolerate Mother
over the summer and be back here away from her before
I knew it. I took a picture of my friend which developed

in sixty seconds and John signed it: "Good luck over the vacation. See you up at camp in the fall." We were all to meet at a Marist campgrounds in September. I could hardly wait. My world was finally beginning to yield the fruit of joy and happiness for which I had longed. Then, in the moment I expected it least, the blow struck. I was summoned to Brother Master's office!

First I stood trembling by his large oak desk. Then he told me to be seated. I could tell Brother Dennis was not pleased with me. I was terrified. His gold crucifix glittered in the sunlight, reminding me that whatever he said was to be accepted as if it came from the Lord. Indeed, as I had been exhorted so many times before, I "knew" that it did. Beads of perspiration appeared on my forehead.

Brother Dennis began calmly: "The brethren have decided that you should not return next year. We do not believe that you are suited to the Marist life. Thank you very much for listening. You are dismissed." My dreams were shattered in fragments around my feet, and I was never to piece them together again, nor take them with me from that office. I sat paralyzed, filled with anxiety. In a moment, reality had come crashing down on my shoulders with a weight I could not bear. On top of this, Mother was on her way to pick me up for the summer. I could do nothing more than say, "Yes, Brother, thank you for this exhortation," then turn and slowly walk down the hall, trying to hide my shame and fate from the happy students who rushed by me, busy with packing and preparing for their summer vacations.

Desperately, I tried to find John. He would understand. A few moments alone with him wouldn't be too much for God to give me. I needed a mercy drink. I had to talk with him, at least for a minute. Running from the main monastery building to the classroom hall I crossed a narrow walkway and bumped into a woman visitor. She turned and looked me square in the eyes. It was Mom!

Realizing that it was over for me, I gave up without a struggle and told her what Brother Dennis had just said about my not returning next year. She said, "I knew this was going to happen. Meet me in front of the monastery. I have the car parked there."

Charging into the dorm, I threw my last few pieces of shaving gear into the trunk. With these articles I packed the beautiful marble statue of the dead Christ in Mary's arms that Mom had given me for Christmas, and the picture of John I still had in my shirt pocket. Eluding the other students by exiting through the hallway closet door, I slowly sank into my seat beside Mother in the car.

Not more than a minute passed before the battle began. "I knew you couldn't make it," Mom opened. "I have already told your brother that if you give me any back talk from now on he is to help me discipline you." Chip had grown into a much more muscular person than I had. Though my original love for him had not diminished during the years, he seemed to like me less and less as time went on. He would prove a good disciplinarian. On and on Mom chattered about why I had been asked to leave the monastery (although she didn't really know herself) and about how I was doomed to severe bodily injury from Chip if I gave her any trouble.

Since I connected God's grace with the sacraments, I felt helpless and despondent. Prayer was always the "Our Father" or the "Hail Mary." Jesus seemed a thousand miles away. I decided to kill myself!

Speeding along the highway to New Jersey, I kept my

right hand constantly on the door handle. If the road
came close enough to a cliff, I would jump. That place up
there looked good. No, about ten miles away there was a
big curve along a higher cliff. That was the perfect spot.
"So you'd better straighten up and stop talking back to
me in the future. ..." Mom's voice droned somewhere
on the periphery of my consciousness. My place to jump
was coming up. I prepared myself by tensing every
muscle in my body and squeezing the handle hard.

For some reason I couldn't do it. I just couldn't do it. I
thought of Mother right there with me in the car. Even
she would panic. What if I didn't die but just maimed
myself. There were surer ways. I'd wait until we were
home and I was alone.

Opening my suitcase back in my room in Fairlawn, I
wanted to forget. Somehow I would obliterate everything that had happened from my mind. No, I wouldn't
commit suicide, but what would become of me I didn't
know. Then I saw the picture of John. Tears came to my
eyes. Picking it up I hugged it to my breast crying freely.
Racked with sobs, I looked toward the suitcase again. On
top of my clothing stood the marble statue of the dead
Christ I had grown to love. I thought of Jesus dead in His
mother's arms. That was easy for Him, I mused. He
could stand up against anybody. He could even keep the
law perfectly. He was God. But what of me? I was no
saint, no spiritual athlete, no diety. How could I ever be
expected to live for God myself?

All the frustration of self-effort and striving coalesced
with my hatred for my mother. I couldn't believe her
hardness, her lack of concern for my feelings, my pain,
my dreams, and aspirations. God, Mother, Brother
Master—they were all the same, always holding stan-

dards higher than I could ever attain and promising hell or punishment for failure.

Clutching the statue firmly in my right hand I swung my arm up over my shoulder, summoning all the strength I could muster, and threw it squarely at the crucifix on the bedroom wall. Smashing into a million pieces, it shattered on the floor. Every effort I made to keep the law seemed doomed to constant, ceaseless failure. From here on it was me alone. If the law of God and man could not be kept, then damn them to eternal hell. I'd cease the struggle and live for whatever pleasure life might hold apart from priest or parent, God or law, for who could meet such heavy demands?

3
The War Years

Returning home from the monastery meant that I was to attend Fairlawn High School for my senior year. This was accomplished in "automatic." I cared little about what I was doing in my classes or with my life in general. If I could not be in the right situation to learn holiness, what difference did it make how I lived? I certainly didn't have it within me to live a godly life on my own.

Alcohol was not easy to obtain in New Jersey when you were under twenty-one, yet Barry, a fellow student at school, took care of this problem for all of us. He could obtain scotch and gin quicker than anyone I ever met. Partly because his parents held liquor in high esteem and partly because he was an excellent thief, we were seldom without it.

Our plan for the year was quickly made. We established a cache of alcohol by the railroad tracks about midway between the high school and my house. Each day we would go out to the proper railroad tie where it was hidden and drink ourselves into a lethargic state. Then we would cut our first class and rendezvous with some other seniors of similar habits at a diner in the Radburn Shopping Center. There we spent hours ventilating our hostile feelings toward those in authority over us, daydreaming about how things would be better once we left home after graduation and were finally on our own.

What motivated me to go out for track that year, I never knew. Does one really need a reason? At five feet four inches tall, one hundred and sixteen pounds, with short legs and a long trunk, I was never destined to be an Olympic decathlon star. Nor did my steady intake of alcohol fit me for the team. Still it was something to do in the afternoon, away from the house and any hassle that might flare up with the folks. So I joined the other track enthusiasts and concentrated on learning the techniques of running low hurdles.

Dennis Brink was a real athlete. He not only knew how to run the hurdles, he actually took part in school competition. A senior, he had been on the team in his junior year as well, and glided over the low gates like a gazelle. Although I never really expected to compete as Dennis did, for some reason I felt compelled to master the event. Who knew? Maybe in college, with a few added inches, I could at least have the joy of participation, even if not the thrill of victory. Hoping to increase my skill, I asked Denny to assist me in pacing.

For the first time that I could recall, a person responded to me in a way that I could really understand. Dennis was warm and friendly, not arrogant or domineering. He knew what he was saying, but never tried to put himself forward as "cool" or to be envied. He gave me of his time freely and spontaneously. I never seemed to be bothering him when I required a second explanation. He appeared genuinely concerned with my learning what I had asked him to teach me, and for no other reason than that I had requested help from him. I knew that he must realize that I wasn't worth the trouble and would never excel at hurdles, yet he remained eager and willing to be both an instructor and a friend.

Yes, Denny was something else! I couldn't believe how thoughtful he was. None of the guys at the monastery were as loving as he, not even John. I just couldn't shake the thought of him from my mind. He never spoke about religion and seemed to be a pretty normal guy. For the first time in my life, I began to feel an emotion coming over me that I could not explain. It haunted me, and I couldn't fight it off.

Entering school one morning, I wondered what Dennis was doing. Suddenly, I felt overwhelmed, almost possessed, by a curiosity, a desire, to know exactly where he was and precisely what he was doing. Checking the master schedule in the principal's office, I found his class. Standing in the hallway I peered through his classroom door. There he was! Soon I was fanticizing about his kindnesses to me, recalling each one individually. Terribly attracted to him, I wanted to be near him, perhaps even to hold him or to be held by him, to tap something of the love which exuded from him, so that it would permeate me in the same manner it did him. He seemed to have every quality I lacked. I needed him, and desperately wanted to get to know him better.

After classes ended one afternoon, I rode away from the school with Chip. He had bought an old car, but to

him it was more precious than gold. Cheryl, his girl-
friend, seemed to admire it as much as he did, only not in
so mechanical and clinical a manner. Even to me, it was a
prestigious thing at the time to drive away from the high
school at the sound of the bell in a flurry of tire squeals
and rubber marks. Finding our way from the lot that day,
I began to question Chip about his relationship with
Cheryl.

It wasn't long before the horrible recognition crept
over me. Each separate aspect of Chip's feelings for her
were exactly those I held for Dennis! The parallels were
inescapable. I had never really thought about the word
"gay" before. Yet in a flash, without diagnostic test or a
counselor's consultation, I realized without a doubt that I
was a homosexual. I desired the same relationship with
Dennis, and had the same feelings for him that Chip had
for Cheryl.

A few moments after this realization struck me, I asked
Chip to drop me off at the library. Reading everything on
homosexuality I could get my hands on there (so that
books speaking of such a thing would not be found in my
room at home), I began to receive my first education into
the intricacies of gay life.

Truly, I was horrified by what I read. I hadn't asked to
be gay, yet I knew that I was. It was not just a high school
crush that burned in my heart like some teenagers
experienced towards their teachers. It was love, erotic
love for a guy. No woman could ever satisfy this desire. It
was emotional, psychological, physical, and sexual.
There was no denying it, nor fighting it. I had to know if
Dennis felt as I did. Perhaps this would explain his kindness to me.

Squeezing through a gate, after the three o'clock bell

had rung for classes to end, I ran two blocks to the track. Passing through the tiers of bleacher seats, I scanned the field and found that practice had been called off. Turning away toward the same gate through which I had just come, I began to walk slowly toward home, when about thirty feet in front of me, I saw him!

Denny and a girl I had never seen him with before stood clutched in a deep embrace, hugging and kissing one another passionately for all the world to see. Hurt, rejected, and humiliated, yet somehow more full of admiration than ever for Dennis because he was "straight," I ducked behind a fence, and headed for home.

The Order of the Most Holy Trinity

The rest of my senior year finally disappeared into the oblivion of yesterdays I had fervently hoped that it would. I'd quit the track team months before, fearing that Dennis might discover my homosexuality. The past few weeks revealed the fact I could push my love for him deep down into the depths of my being, so far, in fact, that I couldn't even remember the feelings that were associated with it very well.

Unbelievably, even to me, a new resolution to try monastic life once again had pervaded my consciousness lately. Somehow, I seemed to feel that I needed God more than ever, now that I had discovered my homosexuality. To become involved in a gay lifestyle was unthinkable. It was sin! Every Catholic knew that. Besides, I realized in those excruciating months since I had left the track team, that religion was as much a real part of myself as gayness. The best and safest place for me seemed to be the monastery. If I was to learn to overcome my deep desire for involvement with a guy, I had to go back and learn how from the monks. Once again, I picked up the *Catholic Directory*. Once again I began to search for just the right community.

My earlier resolutions not to turn to anyone for help had prevented me from venturing into the area of religious involvement for some time. Still feeling somewhat burned by that experience, I was much more careful in observing the various religious orders this time. My first choice, of course, was the Trappists. Yet, in the end, this community took second place to an order which combined something of the active life I had known in the monastery previously with something of the monastic ideals that the Trappists maintained. I thought that perhaps an order combining both prayer and work, both liturgical celebration and social relationship, would be best. Thus I picked the Trinitarians this time.

The Order of the Most Holy Trinity was founded in 1164 by a monk named John De Matha. We were told that he had been in the apostolate of ransoming himself for Christians taken by the Muslims in the Crusades. As the practice of ransom and of holy war both ceased, the Trinitarian monks had turned to other pursuits in an attempt to live out the ideals of Christian service.

Saint John De Matha Catholic High School was the first place of training for postulants seeking a place in the order. We would live in the monastery building and work in one capacity or another assisting the priests in whatever ways we could.

Entering the monastery building, I was immediately struck by the monastic arrangement of the place. The refectory, or dining hall, was formal with long tables set in much the same manner as they had been during my months with the Marists. The superiors sat at the head, the monks in minor orders farther down, and eventually the novices and postulants toward the kitchen. Trinitarian nuns prepared all the meals and served them in an opening in the wall at the far end of the dining hall.

Dorms were located on the second floor. There we all slept, about thirty to a room. The chapel had choir stalls with large throne-like wooden structures similar to those of the Trappists. Along the outside of the monastery building were narrow porches where brothers in training could rest or meditate between liturgical exercises.

Our superior was a young, newly ordained priest whom all of us liked instantly. He was much less pompous than any of the monks I had known thus far, and even smiled occasionally at some of our many questions. Father Vincent was the kind of guy you could even grow to love, given the right situation. I wondered if that would ever arise. The thought of having a simple and holy friendship with one of these monks actually seemed humorous to me. But then you never know, miracles could happen, and perhaps the Lord would allow us postulants some measure of openness, spontaneity, and individual personal relationship. Of course, there would be Father Lupo to contend with before that could happen!

Father Joseph Lupo was the instant enemy of every young monk who entered the monastery that year. He was in his fifties, gray-haired, and had a large pot belly. He had traveled around the world doing whatever military chaplains do. His angry outbursts, self-centeredness, and use of authority and position as a manipulative weapon against those he didn't like were instantly recognized. Everyone, especially those of us at the bottom of the pecking order, realized he was the monk to be avoided if we ever wished to take vows.

Obtaining my first work assignment from Father Vincent, my superior, should have been a premonition of things to come. But I failed to take it as such. I was to be Father Lupo's right-hand man. My job would be to assist him in the vocations office that he had set up at Saint John De Matha Catholic High School next door.

Reporting to Lupo as directed, I found myself sweating profusely in the intense July heat of that Maryland summer. There was no air-conditioning. The building was empty of the students who had crammed its hallways during the winter term. Even if one of the young people had dropped around for a quick game of basketball on the tarred parking lot courts, we were informed that all conversation with them was forbidden.

Father commanded me to type letters on a semi-automatic typesetter down the hall. I had never run such a machine before. It took me some time to put the paper in properly, watch the machine whirr away, and prepare the envelopes for mailing. At the bottom of each letter, a place was reserved for Father Lupo's signature, making it appear that he had typed each one personally. Two or three of the letters had slight spacial errors at first, but nothing that would prevent them from being used, I thought.

As noontime approached, I was informed by the priest that he would have lunch in his office. Running over to the main monastery building, I ordered his lunch from the nuns. Back at the school once again, I arranged the food carefully on his desk, just the way I thought he would like it. Father ate and so far everything appeared to be going well. I wondered if, perhaps, the other monks had been wrong about him.

At five o'clock in the afternoon, when work ended, I

took the fruit of my day's labor to Father Lupo for his inspection and signatures. Observing the huge stack of correspondence, I was proud of what I had accomplished in the heat of that tiring morning and afternoon.

"Do you expect me to send these letters?" the dissatisfied priest exploded. "Look at this! Look at this spacing!" Horrified, I rushed forward to observe the awful mistakes that he must be pointing out. Yet, instead of learning that I had ruined all of the correspondence in some unknown way, I saw him gesturing wildly at one of the first three letters that had been done as I adjusted to the typesetter earlier that morning. I began to offer apologies and assistance in redoing the few letters with poor spacing, but just then I caught a glimpse of his enraged eyes. I froze. He threw the entire stack of letters at me, ordered me to retype them correctly, and stalked from the room, slamming the door behind him on his way out. I was petrified!

Setting the work on the desk, I hurriedly left the school building and rushed to the dorm. Lying on my bed, I cried bitter tears of understanding! The handwriting was on the wall. I would never become a monk! It was only a matter of time until I would be rejected in an arbitrary fashion by this order as well. Yet there might still be a way to avoid the inevitable. Father Lupo was not my superior—Father Vincent was. I could appeal my case to Vincent prior to being scuttled from the postulant program by Lupo. Running down the highly waxed hallway, I skidded to a stop in front of my director's office and took a deep breath.

As I begged Father Vincent to hear me, he motioned me to sit down in a chair. Almost paralyzed with fear, afraid to try to justify myself, I related the events of the day to Father Superior as best I could. Finally I threw myself at his mercy, pleading to be released from Father Lupo's work and assigned somewhere else—if, of course, I would be allowed to stay at the monastery at all after the scene that had just transpired in the school office.

Father Vincent laughed. "You've had a hard first day, kid. Don't be afraid," he said. "Father Lupo is like that. We'll assign you to cleaning out the attic and keep you out of his way as long as we can. This won't be held against you." I relaxed a bit, realizing that I'd over-reacted. Father Vincent understood. My place in the postulant class was still secure. Calming down, I thanked this kind monk for his help, not knowing at the moment that indeed my premonitions had been correct. Only Father Vincent stood between me and dismissal from the order by Father Lupo some time later.

The weeks passed. I began to relish the liturgy of the Trinitarian Community. Both priests and brothers were allowed to chant the office. Here it was mostly in Latin. Still, the praises of the Psalms ascended before the Lord begging for His grace and mercy. Somehow, I didn't know why, I began to believe that God was hearing us. We were interceding for all the sinners of the world. Hour after hour, day after day, those petitions were raised to God:

> Have mercy on us, O God. Hear our prayers, O Lord. We praise You, we worship You, we adore You, O King of heaven and all the earth. Listen to us, O God of heaven. We acknowledge our sinfulness. We pray Your grace and strength upon us.

These were prayers I couldn't deny were the substance and feeling of my heart. As always, my soul was refreshed as I cried for mercy to God for myself and other sinners of the world.

One day not long after these constant prayers had begun to calm my anxious spirit, we were brought together in a conference room by Father Vincent. He was obviously upset and shaken. Taking my place close to the front, near this man I had come to admire and respect, I realized something had happened which would affect all thirty of us postulants, something very serious.

Father Vincent's tone was somber. The entire class was to be sent to the major monastery in Pikesville, Maryland. Here we would work in a new vocations office under the direct supervision of Father Lupo alone. Some friction had developed between the two priests because of Father Lupo's claim that we had not been attending to our work with diligence. Father Abbot at the Motherhouse, Sacred Heart, had received a phone call from Lupo. No longer would Father Vincent be our superior. He had been relieved of his duties as Postulant Master. The abbot had acceded to the request of Father Joseph to place us under his own direct supervision.

A hush ran through the class. We knew that we were finished. Few of us would ever survive under Lupo's direction to take our vows. Dreams were being dashed to pieces all over the room in the hearts of the young monks-to-be. But suddenly anger began to boil up from each. Why? This was the question of the moment. Why had Lupo been allowed to do this? The abbot must have been aware of his manipulation and angry temper. It wasn't fair to put the future of almost thirty postulants in the hands of such a neurotic and unstable man.

For the first time in my experience in a monastery, postulants began to fight back against the injustices of the monastic system which gave such power over our lives to one as cruel and feared as Father Joseph.

Some of us decided to call ourselves "Tricky Lobo's Wolverines." Father Lupo (whose name in Italian is a form of the word "wolf") was our director, all right, but we would be the "Wolverines." We would be the shock troops of the postulant class. We would follow his every move, plot and chart his every action. We would no longer allow ourselves to be terrorized by Lupo without fighting back. The battle was on. The Wolverines were set. The Wolf never suspected a thing!

Our first plan was to let the monks at Saint John De Matha know that we were not going down without a struggle. As the bus pulled up to transport us all down to Sacred Heart Monastery in Pikesville, we planned our first overt operation. Filing onto the bus, we slowly passed the word. We'd sing prison songs all the way to the new monastery. The Wolverines would begin, all others were to follow. We commenced before Lupo ever boarded the bus. "I've Been Working on the Chain Gang" rose loud and clear, floating across the yard and through the open windows of the solemnly ordained clerics busy at their studies on the second floor. At window after window smiling faces appeared. Some of the clerics flashed victory signs to us. They recognized what we were doing: Defiance had won their loyalty. We knew they could be counted on later, if the going got rough. Yet Lupo never understood. The war cry had been raised in his very presence. We would all be dropped from the postulant class under his neurotic supervision. But we would be united affirming each other.

My job at Sacred Heart was to go through all the newspapers from Washington, D.C., and cut out the obituary notices of everyone who had been buried in a Catholic cemetery after a Catholic mass in any of the city's churches. These people would immediately be sent letters of condolence, although we had never met them and knew none of them personally. Nor did we care to. I couldn't believe it! This was an underhanded tactic to raise funds, if I'd ever seen one. I hated and detested the job, but I knew that anything I said about my abhorrence of it would be considered automatic reason for my dismissal by Lupo on the grounds of being unsubmissive. So I grinned and bore it, finding more fuel for the next meeting of the Wolverines.

Hurrying along the novitiate hallway to assemble the entire Wolverine group, I spied Brother Brian sauntering toward me about sixty feet down the long corridor, repeating the dagger scene from *Macbeth*. He was not allowed to speak in the novitiate; nevertheless, he was doing so anyway. A real character, he was one brother who could be counted on to support the Wolverine cause. Suddenly, I saw the abbot twenty feet behind Brian, turning toward him in the corridor from an adjoining passagway. To be caught speaking in the novitiate would mean instant punishment, perhaps an hour or more at prayer on his knees in the chapel reciting the rosary over and over. I angled myself exactly in front of him, though still some distance away, and pointed so that Father Abbot couldn't see. "Behind you!" I formed the words with my mouth, yet without speaking. "Quick, the enemy behind you!"

Brian took a quick glance over his shoulder. Discovering his predicament, he froze. Father Abbot had already heard him. There was no point in stopping now. Carefully, backing all the way down the long hallway in the direction of the oncoming abbot, he simply continued to quote the dagger scene in reverse, and dramatically: "I guess this is not a dagger that I see before me, its handle pointing toward my hand." As he continued the soliloquy, walking in reverse and reversing the entire narrative, he suddenly rushed through an open hallway door and disappeared.

Father Abbot seldom dealt directly with the postulants, and, not having seen his face, could not distinguish which one of the new young men had dared to break monastic custom. He turned around slowly and walked down the corridor from the direction he had originally come, obviously irritated by the entire affair.

Chuckling to myself about this anarchy in these formal monastic hallways, I returned to my cell and began to think. The room contained nothing but a bed, desk, chair, and sink. I seated myself and began to meditate on my reasons for being at the monastery.

Obviously, I hadn't come here without religious ideals. I still deeply wanted to commit myself to the service of the church and learn how to live the demands of true spirituality. Yet I realized that only those more mature than I could lead the way. Only they could help me discover the secrets of holiness. Obviously, this could not happen as a postulant. Father Lupo's work schedule and personal attitude made sure of that.

What was to have been a time of training for true identification with Christ, or so I thought, had fallen into shambles—a battle of postulant class against superior. There was no hope for the situation to be rectified until I reached the novitiate the following year. Then we would have a new director, hopefully one who could relate the facts of godly living with some degree of understanding and concern. Then we would meet a man who cared about our souls.

Until that time, it was war. Tricky Lobo against the Wolverines. If our postulancy was to be completed and the novitiate ever attained, this war would somehow enable us to maintain whatever semblance of justice we could find within the monastery. Only this war could knit us together into a community. We needed a central point of mutual concern for one another if our hopes were to be realized. If we didn't make it through postulancy, none of us would ever become monks. The risk was high. We could be asked to leave at any time if we made a mistake. If we were caught, our future in the order would never be realized. We would be cast aside as unworthy of becoming novices. The secrets of true spirituality would be closed to us forever.

Gathering together all my thoughts, along with the hatred I was beginning to experience for Lupo, we planned the next venture—our rat episode. We had discovered a dead rat among the furniture of an old building that some of the postulants had been ordered to clear out. This would be our gift to Lupo, a present accurately symbolizing our growing animosity toward this despiteful monk.

During the meeting, Brother Luke offered to take the key role in the plan. He alone among us was trusted by Lupo. He alone could bring the rat, wrapped in beautiful paper with a large pink bow, up to Lupo's desk. He alone would not be suspect when the rotting creature was seen in a tissue padded box. The group nodded approvingly. Luke would do it. The Wolverines would strike again!

And so they did. But not without dire consequences. The assembly was convened. Ten Wolverines were requested to leave at once. The rest of us were severely rebuked by Father Abbot. "Never again," he shouted. "Never again will such uncharitable behavior be seen in this house of priests and brothers!" Never again would this happen if we knew what was good for us! Such behavior would cease at once!

Armed by the new and deeper hostility which had grown in our hearts because ten Wolverines had been asked to leave, we held our *own* assembly. Our next attack would occur on September 10. Father Joseph had invited many benefactors of the monastery to Washington, D.C. They would come to the cloistered grounds for a twilight mass.

Instead of being allowed to receive our postulant's habits or robes earlier, as we had expected, we were denied this privilege. Father Lupo had seen to that. Yet now that September 10 had approached, he changed his mind. He would issue our robes for that day only, so that we would look "holy" to the assembled guests. This was too much for our group of monks-to-be, who realized the hypocrisy it represented.

We planned our strategy carefully. Each brother had been assigned a group of benefactors to escort from the outside mass, celebrated by the Archbishop of Baltimore, to the waiting buses. These individual solemn processions would provide a joyful and holy finale to a day spent amidst the monks by their benefactors. When they least expected it, we would move in for the *coup de grace*. Hopefully, it might even mean Father Lupo's transfer itself!

Things worked out better than we had ever dreamed. Most of the buses were delayed outside the city limits of Washington because they had no touring permits. Father

Lupo had forgotten to obtain them. Hot and exhausted in the autumn heat of Washington, the visitors were angry and irritated when they arrived. Still each person went through the ritual of the mass and seemed happy for the tender care of the Wolverines after their long ordeal in the buses. Finally, they quieted down. As the last rays of sunlight disappeared over the hills of the west, we took our places beside the column of twelve or so persons assigned to each of us. We were supposed to march to the buses in silent procession. The only light available was provided by the large artificial flashlight "candle" each Wolverine held high. The procession began. Brian walked by my side. We exchanged knowing glances, then proceeded according to our plan.

Instead of joining the main procession, we took our group of groping pilgrims around to the back side of the mountain. We pushed on through briars and brambles, and spent a very slow, and not-so-holy time before the pigsty. Each follower gasped for breath, and held his/her nose to avoid the awful stench that came from the pigs. Over and over, around and around, the mountainous terrain we walked, until we finally arrived at the swimming pool. Brian glanced over at me. "Okay?" he gestured with his eyes. "Okay!" I affirmed. One after another, the visitors plunged after us into the three-foot deep wading pool. Drenched and cold, they scrambled to its side, shouting for Lupo. Of course, Brian and I had arranged to dim our flashlights, assuring the fact that we would be seen as helpless fellow sufferers of this cruel immersion.

The plan worked perfectly. Excitedly, Brother Brian called me over to the solid oak door where all the remaining fellow Wolverines were clustered. The abbot screamed furiously at Father Joseph. "How could you do this to me, Joe? How could you? It's a disaster—a financial disaster! And the pool, Joe. How could you do this to me?"

We shook our hands and slapped one another on the back, making sure not to create a sound. The Wolf was dead. The Wolverines had triumphed, or so it seemed to us. For it was a sad Father Joseph that emerged from the conference with Father Abbot that day. Yet not so sad that he could forget the war. "Those Wolverines were involved in this somehow," he muttered, as he sauntered from his office down to the chapel to do penance for the September 10 disaster.

Much to our surprise, the abbot had *not* transferred Father Joseph. The Wolf rose from the ashes of the September 10 fiasco more determined than ever to see the Wolverines devastated. And so we were. In the next three months all of us except one were asked to leave. Whatever happened to Brother Brian, I will never know. I imagine that he still recites the dagger scene from *Macbeth* in the novitiate hallways to this day, remembering the time the Wolverines went down fighting the Wolf.

The Larger War

It was hard to believe that only six months had transpired since entering the Trinitarians, I thought, as I traveled back to Fairlawn on the Greyhound bus. The three-hour trip was painful, but I was growing more hardened and callous. I accepted the decision of the superior that I should leave the Trinitarians with ease. This time I realized that the real tragedy would have been for me to stay. Those monks knew nothing of the monastic ideals written about so vividly in the works of Thomas Merton.

They were immature; in many ways simply children. My respect for contemporary Catholic religious life was diminishing with each encounter I had among those who claimed to know the way and be living godly lives.

Turning my attention to the future, I was deeply perplexed. Although I had been accepted by several colleges prior to admission into the Trinitarian Order and completion of high school six months before, I realized that involvement in further academic pursuits was definitely not what I desired. My one aim in life was to get myself together in the context of Christian community. Still, for a Catholic in a pre-Vatican II church, this was impossible. Christian community was equated with monastic living. Since monastic religious life was out of the question for me now, I abandoned this ideal.

My homosexuality had caused me no problems in the monastic environment. I simply had lied to those around me, maintaining a veneer of respectability with those among whom I lived. Though some people probably knew of my gayness, or suspected it, this aspect of my personality never really became an issue. I simply knew that involvement in homosexual acts was wrong, and being a nonaggressive, noneffeminant gay, I covered it over as best I could. This "closet" brand of covert sexual deviance seemed to satisfy everyone. Although I was never truly happy with my sexual feelings, as long as I simply suppressed them whenever they loomed their ugly heads, I felt confident that I could make it in life without much interference from them. Never, since my encounter with Dennis a year and a half before, had they ever seemed to control me in any way. So, I was "safe."

Still, I recognized that my loneliness had to find some place of adequate involvement. It could be overcome best in the communal lifestyle, I thought, so probably whichever way I determined to live in the future, I would always be conditioned at least in part by a desire to overcome loneliness through communal living.

The next few months in Fairlawn were listless ones. Church excited me little. Nor did anything else. Realizing that I had to make a decision about my future, and that I could not remain at home forever, I decided to join the Navy.

The Vietnam War was in full swing that year of 1967. Being drafted was inevitable unless one was deferred for physical or academic reasons. I had neither obstacle to contend with. Rather than let the government draft me into the Army, I decided to enlist. Perhaps in the Navy medical corps I could remain on the periphery of the brutality and violence this war spewed forth.

The thought of seeking a deferment from the service because of my homosexuality never crossed my mind. Who was going to admit to an enlisted man that you were gay? My parents would disown me. That kind of honesty, with its corresponding price tag, was to much to pay. The Navy it would be.

At the Navy recruiting station in New York, I was informed by an officer that I had passed the necessary tests with ease. Looking around me in the crowded room filled with prospective troops, that didn't seem to be an outstanding accomplishment. It looked to me as if any person passed who could sign his name and breathe without wheezing too severely.

Finally another officer motioned me to his desk. I told him that I wanted to join the medical corps so that I wouldn't have to kill anyone. Smiling, almost gently, he offered me the pen. "Simply sign here," he instructed.

"Since you're enlisting, you have the right to choose any specialty you wish. The medical corps is just fine."

I little realized that with that signature I could be signing my death warrant, but sign it I did. After all, I assured myself, wasn't this the duty of every loyal American citizen? With that procedure accomplished, I was informed that I would leave for the Great Lakes Naval Training Center one week later. I was to appear at the station in exactly seven days. Everything would be taken care of then. I was to bring nothing with me. The government would supply whatever needs I had from that time forward.

Only after signing the appropriate papers did it begin to dawn on me what I had actually done. For the next four years I would have no will of my own. Thoughts of Father Lupo stirred in my consciousness. There would be no escape from whomever I was assigned to work with now. But who cared? What difference did it really make? Life was pretty much a process of adjusting as best you could. I probably wouldn't get killed, being in the Navy, and what difference would it really make if I did?

Prior to leaving the recruitment station, however, I decided to chat with one or two of the other inductees. They grinned broadly as I spoke about joining the Navy to avoid the draft, and choosing the medical corps so that I would not have to kill anyone. A tall black guy, who never gave me his name, laid it out for me straight. "Listen, dude," he ventured with total confidence, "The Navy and the Marine Corps go hand in hand. This is wartime, man. You won't be in the Naval Medical Corps for long. They're diverting all their corpsman into the Marines. You've just put yourself into the thick of it. Good luck!"

My face turned as white as his was black. I had really done it now. Death seemed real and very near. Knowing my signature was on the papers, I couldn't back down. But still some urge for life fought its way into my mind. I had to find a way out of this somehow. I just had to.

Walking slowly out of the building, I began to formulate a plan. I took a crosstown bus to another recruiting station, which was still open. Walking into the office, I informed the officer that I wished to enlist in the Army Medical Corps. Filling out all the appropriate forms I had filled out for the Navy just an hour before, I signed my name to the papers. I was now officially a member of both the Navy and the Army. But, if I could get away with this, I would be in boot camp in the Army long before the Navy realized what had occurred. I thought that my chances for living, though probably slim, would be better in the Army than in the heat of the battle with the Marines, to which I'd been told the Navy would assign me after training. I asked the officer how soon I could leave for boot camp and was relieved when he replied, "In two days." I never heard from the Navy personnel again.

Arriving at Whithall Street Induction Center 48 hours later—one month to date after my dismissal from the monastery, I entered a totally different world. Along with the other volunteers, I was poked, prodded, bled, and tested in every way imaginable. Thoughts of cattle being herded through the gates to slaughter flashed through my mind. At one point, it seemed that I might not be accepted into the armed forces at all. I was only five feet, four inches tall and weighed a mere 116 pounds. After some deliberation about my height, the sergeant, determined not to let any of us escape, merely pushed me through the line with the rest of the recruits, and I was in.

We were given a meager meal of what looked like mud, covering a chef's inability to cook hamburger, in a "restaurant" down the street. I was the only white in the group assigned to the train that would take us to boot camp at Fort Jackson, South Carolina.

Deciding to let my parents in on this new bit of news about my destination, so that my body could be recovered if I didn't make it through initial training, I called Mom. She reacted with her usual passivity to such news flashes from me. "At least you're going south where it's warm." I agreed, we hung up, and I was on my way.

Two days later, we were burning undershirts, toilet paper, and anything else we could find to keep warm in the freezing South Carolina night while waiting to be processed. The little stove provided the only heat we had in our makeshift puptents. Harsh noncommissioned officers treated us like the animals and in my mind I was beginning to envision that we were. I began to operate in automatic once again. Pushing all feelings and thoughts of better things from my consciousness, I simply did whatever I was told. I was nothing; why should I pretend to myself that I was anything else? My feelings or thoughts didn't matter any longer. As I recalled my inability to relate to Mom because of her demands, to the rules of the Marists, and to the Order of Father Joseph, it began to appear to me that I was indeed finding my real place in life amidst the commands of the Army personnel marching us from one place to another. I was alive to serve the wishes of those in authority over me, whomever they might be. I was the "clone," the "android," the man of Aldous Huxley's *1984*, a servant of my master of the moment. And I was beginning to get used to it.

Thus, as we underwent the ancient military rituals of having our heads shaved, our clothing stripped from us as we stood naked, waiting for new issues of underwear, being marched from tent to barracks, and told when to eat, sleep, and go to the bathroom, I offered little resistance. This was life. Everyone simply acceded to the demands that were made on them. I would do the same and become a good soldier, a real man, a performer of the ideals of American citizenship. Mars, the god of war, would be my new master. If I died serving him, at least I would know that I had performed as a young Catholic patriot was supposed to perform. What, after all, did life hold for any man?

I was assigned to Delta Company, second barracks, for basic training. My drill sergeant was a young black non-commissioned officer who was kinder than some I was to meet later. He had the habit of "banging the boots," that is, hitting the trainees on their hard helmets with his long parade stick. He never treated me any differently from the others and was precise and meticulous in his job. He had been through the process of turning "boots" into soldiers many times before. Almost every word he shouted came from the manual used to direct his actions.

At 5:00 a.m. in the cold South Carolina morning we assembled for breakfast in the Army compound. Each platoon of the entire company ran from their barracks, forming proper columns behind the sergeant. We immediately were given the command to sound off, loud and clear, for all the other platoons to hear: "D21—Delta Demons—best damn devils in the bunch, sir." Our DI (drill instructor) would swear, making some derogatory comment about how that couldn't be true, or how we would see that it was today on the rifle range, or at hand-to-hand combat training.

Breakfast was a quick session of forced feeding. We ate in silence, and were immediately sent back to the barracks for cleanup.

About sixty bunks comprised the sleeping furniture of the inductees ("boots"). The floor was waxed and polished to a high shine. We were to make our beds so tight that they would "squeak." This meant no wrinkles, no sags. Our lockers were arranged in exactly the same order as our fellows. This was prescribed by the book, much the same kind of manual that directed our actions in the monastery. Shaving gear went on the left of the top shelf, a towel on the right. The shower room was at the end of the locker. Here all sixty men showered together. We were expected to leave it immaculate for the sergeant's inspection, with the silver faucet knobs gleaming in the sunlight that would appear soon through the windows. The toilets, which had no stalls surrounding them, stood open in long rows along the edge of the latrine. The recruits exchanged filthy stories as they used them.

I decided to take advantage one morning of the ten minutes that I had left, after completing all of my chores, until the sergeant arrived back at the barracks. Being very small, I curled myself up on the top of my footlocker which stood at the end of my bunk, and promptly fell asleep. I had no fear of waking up at the appropriate time. The shouted commands to fall in would sound through the dormitory where I lay. In a moment, I was asleep. In what seemed like the next moment, I was screaming on the floor, pain throbbing through my entire left side. The drill instructor had come in early and kicked me from the locker. I lay sprawled out and clutching my ribs. "Get up!" he commanded loudly. "And stop this loafing!" He added some profusely abusive language as he left the room. A couple of the guys helped me to my feet. Although the wind had been knocked out of me, and my ribs were sore and tender, none of them were broken. I could make it through the strenuous day. So I fell in with the rest of the troops.

Rifles were issued to us. Today we would be engaged in hand-to-hand combat, for the last day of the series. We had been in this training for two weeks. "Fix bayonets!" the DI screamed. "Now tell me," he yelled, "What is the spirit of the bayonet?"

"To kill! To kill! To kill!" the troops responded just as loudly.

I began to feel ill. "To kill! To kill! To kill!" reverberated in my brain, deafening my consciousness, but not totally. I was repulsed! The games were over. Cowboys and Indians, this definitely was not. It was real! I was being trained to kill—to kill with a knife fixed to the end of a 16.5 lb. M-14 rifle. Rebellion emerged from deep within me. I *wouldn't* do it! I *couldn't* do it! It was wrong. I had joined the medical corps to save lives, not to end them. I knew I had to escape, but I didn't know how.

As I tried to get my thoughts together, to make some kind of protest or response to this open fanaticism, this blatant hatred for the enemy, whoever the President of the United States said that he was going to be, I heard the drill instructor yell loudly, "Now, men, you think you're good, don't you? You think two weeks will make you proficient in killing. . . ." (He uttered a string of profanity.) "I'll give it to you straight. If you ever allow the enemy to get close enough for you to use your bayonets, this training you've been through won't save you. You're a dead man."

"You're a dead man," I kept repeating to myself. "The spirit of the bayonet is to kill. You can't kill. You're a dead man. Kid, you're a dead man."

I lined up with the others as we proceeded to the rifle range. I have to put myself in automatic, I told myself. Don't think, don't question, don't feel. Put it into automatic, kid. You'll make it if you don't think about what you're doing. The exercise was completed. The remaining training and boot camp came to an end. And, finally, graduation was behind me. I had done it all without any further reflection. I had submerged my true self for eight weeks. Every time I had begun to think or feel something contrary to what I knew was expected, I simply quit thinking or feeling at all. Each period of depression I rejected, resisted, and did away with. Every twinge of conscience concerning the morality of learning to kill I deadened. Perhaps, indeed, I was learning how to serve this new god, Mars, very well.

The sacrifice of myself during boot camp won respect from my sergeant. My next assignment was at Fort Sam Houston Medical Training Center in San Antonio, Texas. Here I would attend Leadership Training School. Unknown to me, the officers had searched through the records to find those with outstanding academic ability and better-than-average physical capability. Though not large, or ever first in my physical training classes, I was performing better than many. My high IQ scores convinced my superiors that I could handle Leadership Training School. But I soon discovered that there was a deeper reason.

The United States Army had lost so many medical

corpsmen in the Vietnam conflict that they were forced
to rely heavily on student leaders from among the ranks
of the trainees for staffing the training center at Fort Sam
Houston. Men officially still privates were given acting
stripes. They would function in the capacity of a corporal
or sergeant, freeing those who truly held these ranks to
pursue the tasks of the Army at war. I was to assume the
role of corporal for training purposes. That's why they
were sending me to Leadership Training School.

We were called "grapeheads" by the trainees because
of the maroon helmets we wore to set us off from them.
This symbol of authority, along with our training stripes,
was to cause all under us to obey our commands. Our
training period was brief and effective. We could indeed
march troops from place to place with ease. Fighting
men were channeled through us prior to the time they
had to submit to those in real command. This was not a
great position of responsibility, but it was the most
responsible assignment that could have been given to a
man at the bottom of the barrel. I had jumped from E-1
to "Acting E-4," from buck private to acting corporal, in
only a few weeks.

It was during training in our medical classes that I first
became aware of a phantom company—a strange, aloof
group of people who seldom mixed with us except at
meals. These men were somehow different than any I
had ever met. They were generally as serious as we were,
but they smiled spontaneously and enthusiastically from
time to time. And they seemed relaxed, which we seldom
were. They were confident and secure in a way that none
of us usually were.

One day when I had a few hours to myself I sat down
to lunch with one of these soldiers. I questioned him con-

cerning the reason he always kept away from the rest of the medical trainees. He grinned and proceeded to explain the situation. "I belong to the 500 area," Joe (I later learned his name), stated nonchalantly. "We're all conscientious objectors. I myself am a Seventh-Day Adventist. We refuse to carry guns, but will serve in the military in a noncombatant way. That's why we're here in medical training. We have no combat boot camp at all that involves physical violence. We may end up in 'Nam like the rest of you, but if we do, we will *absolutely refuse* to fight. We aren't required to carry a weapon."

Admiration for this man of conviction gripped me deeply. Feelings of revulsion for the bayonet training that I had endured overwhelmed me. "He sure was lucky," I thought, "not to have gone through that." I inquired how he had avoided combatant training in the beginning. "I'm 1-A-O," Joe smiled. "They have three listings: 1-O, which means you will not serve in the Army at all, like Mennonites; 1-A-O, which means that you will serve, but as a noncombatant (that's what I am); and 1-A, which you are," he said. "You're too late now for getting the 1-A-O listing, I think. But, if you really have a thing about fighting, I'll see what I can do for you. Why not come with me to services this Saturday and I'll introduce you to our minister, Captain Johnson?"

Relating my revulsion for the violent training that I had undergone, I decided to take Joe up on his invitation. Even if he was a Protestant, he could still perhaps use his denominational affiliation to get me out of my present predicament of killing others in Vietnam, and risking getting myself shot up as well. We agreed to meet at nine o'clock on Saturday, shook hands, and departed for our respective barracks.

Three days later I met Joe right where he said he would be. I had decided not to accompany him to the Seventh-Day Adventist services, because it would violate my own religious convictions (Catholics were not allowed to attend Protestant services). We met for a late brunch instead. Just as we were ready to leave the canteen after a long exchange of views regarding the immorality of war, a young neatly dressed man sauntered up to the table and asked to join us. Joe smiled in recognition. Captain Johnson, in civilian clothes, seated himself without requesting any salute at all. I was shocked. It was the first time I had actually spoken personally with any man in the Army of a higher rank than my own. I was somewhat reluctant to speak openly to him, but I was ready to listen to what he had to say.

The conversation centered mostly on Captain Johnson's views of war. Oddly enough, right in the mess hall of the combat corpsmen's training center on a Army post, he spoke freely and spontaneously of his deep and abiding hatred for war and conflict. After relating to us his belief that one could heal and not kill, even in the midst of the Vietnam situation, we rose and followed him a block or two to his base chapel. Welcoming us to his sparse but comfortable office, Pastor Johnson (as I had now come to call him) was offering to pray with me, that I would be released from my 1-A status and given a noncombatant rating.

Although I had never prayed with a Protestant before, nor spoken personally with a minister other than a Catholic priest, I seemed unable to say no to him. He was still a captain in the Army in my mind, and I hesitated to buck him in any way. He was my master of the moment. Nodding for him to go ahead, I thought he would mumble an "Our Father," possibly with a different ending than what I was used to, and nothing more. But such was not the case.

Captain Johnson took off his coat, knelt right on the floor of his office, and lifted his hands high into the air. This seemed terribly strange to me, and I couldn't bring myself to imitate his physical posture completely. I simply knelt and bowed my head. "O Lord," he began, "we come before You to give You praise and glory, and ask that You would hear the prayers of Your servant that Kevin might not have to become involved with the weapons of war. Rather, Father, make him a channel of healing, cleansing, and strengthening to those wounded by the snares of Satan and the hatred and hostility of men." There was absolutely no denying it. *This man knew God!* It was as if he had a direct channel to heaven! He spoke so freely and spontaneously that I almost envisioned the Lord Himself coming down to stand in our midst. Yet, of course, I concluded that that was impossible.

My mind flashed back to a group of young people I had seen in downtown San Antonio. They had been preaching in the streets and parks. They too seemed to know Jesus like this man did. What was the secret of their power, their easy fellowship and conversation with God? Especially, I wondered at their lack of embarrassment in speaking about the Lord with those not acquainted with their strange but fascinating manner of relating with Him.

Rising from my knees, I thanked Captain Johnson for his prayers, and left Joe and him on the run to get back to the barracks before the next activity of the day. Somehow, I didn't want to leave them. They seemed as if they almost . . . well, it was kind of like, they . . . well, like they *loved me*. Or, at least they cared about me, anyway. I'm probably overreacting, I thought. Besides, they aren't even Catholic! They couldn't know God. Without the sacraments, through which His grace is channeled, they—they must be doomed to hell!

Just a little over a week after having spoken to Joe and to his minister, I was confined to the hospital with an unknown stomach ailment. The doctors punctured me with a long needle through my abdomen to obtain a specimen for examination. I felt as though I was being kicked by a mule. After this, I was free to move around a bit.

I spoke freely and openly with wounded men who had been brought back from Vietnam. They seemed ecstatic to be back; few hesitated to share their experiences. I grew to like them, and became concerned for them in a way that led me to believe that one day I might truly be of some help on the battlefield. I had heart, I thought. I could bring some limited measure of comfort and strength to others. My confidence grew. I was happy to be a medic. I wanted to help the suffering and bring life to mankind.

This initial involvement with the patients gave me a feeling of bravado. Upstairs was the severe burn ward. Few were allowed to enter there. I had helped transport some of the men off the helicopters when they had arrived. I'd go up to the burn unit, I decided, and see how these men who had been receiving the best care that veterans of the war could receive were getting along. I'd try to cheer them up.

Entering the corridor marked "No Visitors," I was not at all prepared for what lay in front of me. Dozens of men lacking ears, noses, eyes, and parts of their limbs lay on

their beds, covered with quilt-like bandages, and surrounded by machinery which whirred and emitted
strange noises into the ward—dozens of pathetically
mangled men lay before me in the throes of death. The
lucky ones had died already. Scanning the broken, bleeding, and partially charred bodies which lay before me, I
could not contain my feelings. I turned to walk away, behind me lay more bodies—bodies of men lacking skin
which should have covered one place or another, one
limb or another, one arm or hand or face or another. Not
a single man smiled. Few seemed conscious at all. I made
it only to the end of the hallway. Sickness, that feeling of
revulsion I had experienced when yelling, "To kill! "To
kill!" in bayonet practice, crept over me. In the bathroom, I vomited continuously until there was absolutely
nothing left in my stomach. Only one thought entered
my mind. For these men, most of whom would be dead
in six weeks, who had won? Who had won the war in
Vietnam? What was victory? What was winning?

For the first time in my life, I had sensed a oneness—a
unity with all men. Beneath race or nationality, beneath
allegiance to king or president, there was a truly common
humanity—a precious something—a being given to us
by God. This and this alone mattered. The thoughts
surfaced so fast I could not contain them. Why, I
thought, I'm a traitor. I would just as soon help a North
Vietnamese soldier who lay broken and battered on the
battlefield as an American one. I had no loyalty, no
honor, no patriotism for my country. In that moment,
Mars was dethroned. I recognized that I, too, had been a
helpless victim of his ploys. I'd enlisted to be an
American soldier, but I was no more a soldier than those
dying an agonizing death in the severe burn unit only

feet away. No, I was not a soldier. I was a . . . a man! A man who longed to help others, to heal, to strengthen, to alleviate suffering and pain. I *had* to find Captain Johnson and Joe. Only they would understand.

Entering the base chapel, I recognized my minister friend immediately. I took him aside and begged for some of his time. He gave it freely, pained himself as I told him what I had seen. Yet, somehow, he was pleased with this answer to his prayer for me. We agreed then and there that I would definitely attempt to obtain a 1-A-O classification. I would never lift a weapon again. If I were sent to 'Nam, I would heal until I died, not kill until we "won" some abstraction of a "victory."

Upon my discharge from the hospital, I was assigned to another medical training unit. Walking into the master sergeant's office, I requested the proper forms to fill out to change my classification. I wanted to become a conscientious objector and nothing could change my mind. Immediately, I was shuttled into a separate room. A twenty-three year-old second lieutenant entered. I was given permission to remain seated. He approached me as if I had two heads. Curious, interested in anything I might have to say. I felt terribly nervous. No one had given me any personal attention since Captain Johnson and Joe. Somehow, I feared this man. I knew I must be careful, telling him only what had to be told. Whatever I said would be held against me.

Briefly, I reviewed the events of my hospital confinement, relating carefully that I believed that there was a common humanity and dignity among all men which could not be denied. "My nationality was not American," I stated. "It was. . . ." I faltered, stammered, sweated. "It was . . . well . . . I was a man!"

The lieutenant's smile turned into a sneer. "A man?" he asked, "You think you're a man?"

Thoughts of my homosexuality came to mind. Did he know? Would this be used against me? I was terrified.

"A *true* man," he continued, "would fight for freedom, for justice, and those things which made life worth living. It's not only the quantity of the years of a man's life that matters," he told me, "but it's the *quality* of the years that count."

I tried to imagine those men in the severe burn unit having a good quality of remaining years.

The lieutenant became somber. He told me that he didn't really like to fight any more than I did. It was just that without defense there was no security. The United States was not involved in an offensive war of aggression. Carefully, he led me down the path of identification with the wonderful South Vietnamese people. He spoke harshly of the "gooks" or North Vietnamese people, who dared to interfere with the free South Vietnamese brothers—killing, plundering, and raping them at will.

I pictured a North Vietnamese soldier lying battered and broken on the battlefield, and tried to imagine what I would do if I saw him. I held my ground. I wouldn't pit a man from the North against one from the South. I wouldn't put one country over another in terms of sovereignty. All men have a dignity of life and should solve their problems without violence or killing.

The lieutenant laughed, and even I squirmed at the ludicrousness of my statement. It all seemed so idealistic, so irrelevant to reality, so idylic. Yet the picture of those dying men in the severe burn unit wouldn't go away. Though some might kill, I would not. Though some might go to war, I would not. Though some might rape and maim and hurt others, I would refuse. No, I was not better than other men, but I was different. Perhaps it even had something to do with my past involvement in religious life, or my homosexuality. Be that as it may, if I was a freak, a weirdo, or kook, so be it. But here and now, I would declare flatly that I would refuse to carry a weapon ever again.

The lieutenant seemed somehow unshaken by my adamancy. It didn't seem to matter to him at all that I wouldn't give in to his logic or persuasion. He smiled a sneerish smile again. "What religion are you, soldier?" he demanded loudly.

"Catholic, sir," I replied.

"Do you realize that the Catholic Church's official teaching about war accepts the validity of a just war under five conditions, all of which are met in terms of the Vietnam conflict?"

"Yes, sir," I replied.

"Well, then, your request for the needed forms to become a conscientious objector is granted, but I will not take up my first sergeant's time in filling them out. Take them with you, but remember that you'll never receive permission to give up your weapon as long as you remain a Catholic. Now get out!"

I exited quickly, grateful that nothing worse than a verbal thrashing had befallen me.

The master sergeant shoved the appropriate forms in front of me. "They all have to be filled out in triplicate," he boomed, his voice alerting everyone in the room that an out-of-order request had been made. I completed the necessary paperwork and left. I never saw the forms again. For the rest of my time in the Army, I was rudely informed that they were lost in Washington each time I requested information regarding their processing.

A short time after my encounter with the first lieutenant and my graduation from medical training, I was reassigned to my first regular duty station. My job was to become a psychiatric technician, assisting veterans of the Vietnam conflict at the Wilson Army Hospital in Fort Dix, New Jersey. The work was rewarding and informative.

The psychiatric ward was locked, but most of the patients were allowed to move about freely. They had undergone nervous breakdowns on the battlefields. I read their charts. Most had finished high school or trade school. A majority of them had gone for further training in college, obtaining degrees for further technical skills. They were intelligent and articulate. One of them was a medical doctor. They responded swiftly to being out of the combat situation. I was told that few, if any would remain nonfunctional after six months away from the horrors of the war in which they had been involved. It seemed there was a direct corollary between the effects of the conflict and the intelligence and sensitivity of the patients. The more astute and aware of them were those who suffered the most. The less perceptive suffered least. Yet all knew that no one could participate in the horrors of 'Nam for long without experiencing severe anguish.

My job on the psychiatric floor was demanding, but challenging. And challenge was something I savored. Here, for the first time for almost six months, I was surrounded by caring professionals. Nurses and doctors put others before themselves, at least on the job. The whole process of hospital involvement seemed something I could really relate to. In meeting the demands of other people, I spent less time pouting over my own problems.

Although I was told that the rate of nervous breakdowns was great among the psych techs themselves, this mattered little to me. I began to volunteer my spare time in the emergency room, working a second shift voluntarily, so that I could pick up whatever techniques I might one day need in 'Nam.

One evening as I was working this shift, I was informed that I should head for the ambulance immediately. All of us technicians in the emergency room took separate shifts unloading the ambulance and it was my turn. I had no idea what I would face this time. Opening the door I saw before me a large man, perhaps six feet, five inches tall, with tensed muscles, hugging his arms, and leaning against the side of the vehicle. I stepped in. Slowly, cautiously, I offered him a cigarette. He accepted. We sat down together for a moment in silence. Then I informed the soldier, a young private, that we would have to leave the ambulance and go inside to the emergency room. He agreed. Leaning on me, as if I were the Rock of Gibraltar, he stumbled along with me to the doctor's station. Gently and carefully, I proceeded with the routine paperwork, letting this troubled man know that I empathized with him and cared about him whatever his problem might be.

Soon the story came tumbling forth. His brother had been killed in Vietnam; he had received the news only that morning. His father had died in the Second World War, and now he felt alone in the world. Two of the persons closest to him had been destroyed in the ravages of war. When I reported these facts to the doctor, he told me to admit the private to the psychiatric floor above. Because I worked the 8:00 a.m. to 4:00 p.m. shift on the psych floor, I knew my way around and was able to help the troubled private with the admission procedures myself. Once on the floor, he told me he was hungry—he hadn't eaten in hours. Although I was not supposed to be in the kitchen so late at night, I did go down to get him a meal. I watched him carefully while he ate, taking all the utensils with me as I left, once he had finished his meal. Returning to the emergency room, I was informed that the soldier I had just befriended had completely wrecked the orderly room of the company to which he was assigned, hurling typewriters, chairs, and desks in this direction and that. Fortunately, none of the army personnel in the room at the time had been severely hurt. I must watch out for him, they warned me, and be careful and alert for trouble whenever I was with him.

I completed my tour of duty for the night and then proceeded, after a hasty cup of coffee, to the psychiatric floor where I worked during the day. My first job was to arouse the patients and get them ready for breakfast. There were no on-and-off flip switches in the rooms. I had the one key which would turn on the lights, illuminating all of the sleeping soldiers.

After turning the lights on, I walked into the room which was occupied by my friend of the evening before. To my surprise, he rushed at me, lifted me entirely off my feet, and apparently intended to hurl me from the seventh-floor window to the top of the emergency room roof below. I was petrified! Not knowing what to say, I simply asked, "Can't we talk this over?" He recognized my voice, set me down, and walked out of the room.

He returned a moment later with a steaming cup of coffee in one hand and a cigarette in the other. "You're the little guy that helped me last night," he said. "I'm sorry, man, I just flipped out. It's been really rough."

For the first time in my life I recognized that it was not the size of a man that really mattered; it was the size of his heart. If I held love in my heart for others, they would respond in some measure in terms of that love. It was a basic principle I wanted to live by from that time on, although I didn't always succeed. I resolved never to be upset again about being only five feet, four inches tall. In relating to other people, even those considered dangerous, I would let them know I loved them. Usually, I decided, they would respond in like measure as I reached out to them.

Because I would not become involved in sexual exploits, like others on the staff, I had much time to myself. I made few friends because of my refusal to participate in what I termed "sinful behavior." In turn, I was rejected and treated as an outcast. But I didn't mind. I was not into dope at that time. The soldier with the bronze star who had offered me grass still remained, in some sense, my friend when I refused. I was beginning to think that I could achieve by myself among the sick in the wards what I had once longed to receive from the monks, the ability to learn how to become a genuinely good and loving man.

As I attempted to show concern for the patients, I was in a definitely superior position. They were suffering, and I was helping to alleviate that suffering. They were dependent, and I was independent. They were hurting, and I was helping. This made me feel great, though I took no pleasure in their suffering. My ego inflated when I realized that I was valuable to the medical care health team. I was respected for my accomplishments. My long hours were noticed. I was becoming a "somebody" in the hospital. As long as I remained in this comfortable situation of always being the one who gave, the one who was healthy and had the answers, I could convince myself that I was, indeed, a worthwhile person.

Filled with this new pride in my achievements, I left the hospital one Saturday morning by bus for home enthused with this sense of coming to life, of coming into my own, that I had so recently discovered. My thoughts were pleasant ones as the bus passed through the countryside, the cities and towns, on its way from Fort Dix to New York, and then, on to Fairlawn. I was unaware that this weekend would change my life and bring me to the brink of hell itself.

I met him at the same diner where I had spent so many hours talking with my friends during my senior year in high school. He was a middle-aged man. The commotion he aroused from the other patrons of the eating establishment seemed to revolve around the fact that he was drunk—stone drunk and boisterous. Someone took a swing at him. He grabbed the counter, and almost fell to the floor, but managed to regain his balance. This nameless drunk began to arouse my sympathy. I would come to his rescue. He couldn't walk far, and I would assist him to his home. I paid my bill and went out of the diner after him, catching him just as he fell against the railing once more.

He motioned in the direction of his house, and we started toward it. I had always hated the smell of alcohol on a man's breath, and this man reeked of the stuff. That only made me more willing to assist him. I recalled that Saint Francis of Assisi had helped those who were unlovely and sinful. It was dark when we arrived at his house a few minutes later. "Wait here," he said. He went around the back of the building and got his key. Opening the door, he told me to be very quiet and invited me in. Unsuspectingly, I followed him.

Once in the basement room that he had used as a bedroom, he seemed to regain his strength. He was a homosexual. He wanted me to engage in a sex act with him. He had determined that I was gay back at the diner. He was not half as drunk as he smelled.

My thoughts raced. Up to this time, I had never become physically involved with another guy, except for a brief period of sexual experimentation with my brother around age eight or nine. The thought of it repulsed me, and yet I had to admit it drew me in an incomprehensible manner I couldn't deny. The situation seemed right; this man was a stranger. I was safely away from the fort, and my parents would never meet him or ever know him. There was no obligation, no strings attached to his request, or so I thought. I could walk away from the encounter and really begin to assess whether the physical act of sex between two men was what I had so fanticised it to be. So I consented.

Once the encounter was finished, the man dropped off to sleep in no time. The sexual session seemed to be a matter of course with him. He simply called it a night and asked me to find my own way out. I never saw him again.

Sauntering across the streets in the early morning of that breaking dawn, I could feel the guilt rising. I felt filthy, scared, alone. I had done something I knew I shouldn't have done. I had compromised my principles; I had sinned. And yet in that compromise an inner drive had simply overwhelmed me. I was powerless, definitely in the grips of something bigger than myself. There were no choices; I "had" to sin. Yet, on the other hand, I was commanded *not* to sin. The law reared its ugly head. I could never fulfill the prescriptions it contained; I was powerless. Although it seemed that a certain part of my conscience knew what was right, I always ended up giving in to sin in the end.

Almost at our house, I tried to rationalize away the sense of guilt I experienced. Homosexuality was wrong only because the Catholic Church said so. If they were wrong on the issue of war, they could be wrong on this as well. Other cultures practically fostered homosexual practices among their people. Ancient Rome and Greece did and they were among the most sophisicated societies the world has ever known. Maybe this whole "guilt thing" was a matter of my being too hard on myself. Maybe, all my religious training had given me an overactive superego. I'd be okay. I'd simply forget it.

But as soon as I got home, I headed for the medicine chest and swallowed every pill I could find. Then I headed for some friends' house to die in their basement in peace. I liked them. The Browns had almost become a substitute family for me, since I remained unable to communicate with the Linehans. They seemed to have all the love that my own family lacked. They would understand, somehow.

Finding my way onto their couch, semiconscious, I grabbed a razor blade from my duffel bag. Slashing myself from shoulder to ankle, the blood dripped freely to the floor, and gathered in little pools. I stood up and began to wander in a lethargic state. Hundreds of slashes crisscrossed my arms and legs. I no longer knew where I was, or what I was doing.

Deciding for the first time since the monastery to pray, I said, "Dear God, you know that I cannot overcome this homosexuality. Yet you also know that it is wrong. Since I cannot overcome it, I will die rather than go on sinning against you, through homosexual sin. You are the only person I know who understands. I'm coming over to you." Just then I passed out on the bathroom floor.

Mrs. Brown apparently called the ambulance which rushed me to a hospital where five surgeons stitched me up from toe to head. Still unconscious, I was transported to the Army hospital at Fort Dix, and then to the one at Valley Forge, Pennsylvania, where I lay in a coma for seven days.

The first sound I heard when I finally awoke was the voice of another patient. He uttered a profanity, followed by the words, "He made it!" The patients had been taking votes on whether I would live or die. Apparently, this patient had lost.

I tried to sit up, but my arms were completely bandaged. Each effort I made to raise myself into a sitting position on the bed caused me intense pain. As the pressure of the sheets on my bandaged arms and legs throbbed and burned, I went into a seizure and passed out once again.

Sometimes later a psychiatrist entered the ward and spoke softly with me, telling me that everything would be all right. I would come out of this thing, and he would help me. I didn't care one way or another. I lost consciousness once more. Horrible dreams of floating images raced through my mind. Imaging myself smashing into a barbed-wire fence over and over, and cutting myself to pieces in the fall, I floated on the outer limits on what seemed like oblivion.

It took me about two weeks to regain any strength at all. Then the psychiatrist asked me to accompany him into his office which adjoined the ward to which I was assigned. He wanted to give me a complete physical examination. But each time he touched me, I drew back in terror. I was unclean, dirty, ashamed. I was not fit to associate with fellow human beings.

Dr. Delsmir asked me if I wished to see my parents. I was horrified. "No!" I exclaimed, "No, I couldn't!" But they were allowed to come anyway. The first thing my mother said when she was alone with me was, "Do you recognize what you're doing to our name in the community?" I couldn't bear this additional guilt. I simply turned and walked away from her, hating her still more for her insensitivity.

The weeks began to pass. I had to decide what I would do. I could stay in the hospital and rot or try again to live up to God's law. The thought of measuring up to God's standard, however, horrified me. I was sure that I could never do it.

Valley Forge Hospital was near John's hometown. We had known each other in the juniorate many years before, and I hadn't seen him in a long time. I decided to call him. We spoke for a while. He promised to share with me again sometime later on. As we hung up, I felt rejected, alone, surrounded by the demands of others, and now of myself, which I could not fulfill. To live or to die—did it really matter? Which had the more meaning? Certainly life didn't have much.

Then it happened. One day, as I walked along the pathway of the garden at the hospital, I caught a glimpse of someone I knew. It was John! He had not forgotten about me after all. Hurrying back to the ward, I greeted him as he entered. We went to the day room and sat down. "Here's some food," he said, pointing to the big box of chocolates, "and there's the cigarettes." He placed a pack of Winstons on the table. "I want to hear about it," he continued. "Tell me everything."

Hour after hour the torrent lasted. I spilled forth all of my pain and frustration—the shattering of my dreams to live a truly Christian life, the overwhelming power of the homosexual drive, the hopelessness and despair of attempting to please those who seemed to expect so much of me, when I always seemed to be able to give so little. I never remembered a word he said. It didn't seem important. I don't think he had any answers. But he was there, and he loved me, and that was enough.

"I'll pick you up on Saturday," he announced matter-of-factly as he walked from the hospital ward. "You don't belong in a place like this. Be ready, I'll come around nine o'clock." I didn't even know whether I could get a pass that Saturday. Since I had no place to go anyway, I had never attempted to try for one in the month that I was hospitalized. Dr. Delsmir consented and new hope surged within me. The friendship that I had once made so long ago in the juniorate to help me in a time of trouble was being continued. I had believed then that somehow John could be counted on to care. And now, so many years after we had parted at the monastery, we began to discover together what real love is all about.

I spent the following weekend with him driving through the Pennsylvania countryside, observing the beautifully colored trees, and listening with intense interest why he had left the Marists himself. He said it was rebellion, pure and simple. The structured life of a monastery had finally taken its toll. Injustices arose and he left. That was all he would say. How grateful I was that in leaving the seclusion of the religious order he had become available to meet me, at my point of suffering, in the real world. It was an encounter that was worth more to me than all the prayers we had ever prayed, and all the penances we had ever done.

About two weeks later, I made an important decision. My thoughts had turned to God once more. I began to realize that life without Him had no meaning at all. Outside of the Lord's will lay only chaos and destruction. I would give the world another chance. I'd try again with the recognition that Jesus was God, and though I didn't understand how to relate to Him, still He was God, wasn't He? Well, I'd make a leap of faith, a sort of jump into the wilderness of believing that He was. Trusting in Him, I could believe that life had meaning, and search for a way of realizing it in my own experience one day. Actually, this assent was not so much one of faith as it was one of hope. Hope always seemed to get me through when all else failed.

Mom didn't seem very pleased to see me again. She consented to allow me to return home only if I placed myself under the care of a Freudian psychoanalyst. This physician really did little to assist me. How could I share with him where I was at in my heart when he would tell my parents? I feared them greatly. By this time, they'd began to fear me as well. What if I tried something stupid again like I had before. What if I did something terrible to them?

As I continued to see the psychiatrist of their choice, I selected a job of my own. New York University hired me to grade papers in the office of their Psychological Services Center. It didn't pay much, but it was a job, and I enjoyed it.

One Friday when I returned home to Fairlawn after

work, my mother told me that she and Dad and I were going to the summer home for a weekend at the Jersey shore. They had purchased a house there many years before, and each week they retreated to the peace and tranquility of their little hideaway. I didn't want to go. I still needed to be alone, or perhaps with a friend or two. I felt pressured when she threatened to call the police if I didn't go along with her plans.

I could tell that she was scared—scared that I would once again attempt to harm myself in the large house, all alone. I assured her that I was fine. She wouldn't listen, and the argument became louder. My father rushed down the stairs and attempted to beat me onto my knees in front of her. He ordered me not to talk back to her, which truly I had not done. I was terrified. Grabbing my coat and wallet, while pushing my father away from me, I left the house never to return. The black eye that I received from Dad sealed a breach in our relationship that time never healed.

4

No Bread in the Wilderness

The Society of Friends

Crossing over the George Washington Bridge after the encounter with my parents that had left our relationship "irreconcilable," I attempted to gather my thoughts together. I could rely on my job at the Testing Office of New York University for financial support, but I had only a few dollars in my pocket at the moment. This was not enough for a room for the night. I was scared. My sole hope seemed to lie in building my future, at least for a time, around my work. There I could discuss my problems with my fellow employees and plan some sort of arrangement regarding a place to live.

Dejectedly, I shuffled into the office where I met Sharon and Carol who were both surprised to see me on a Saturday when I didn't have to work. They noticed how upset I was and immediately inquired why I was so depressed. I recounted the events of the day, placing special emphasis on the fact that I was now homeless, and

they seemed to understand. They were both quite
worldly and had been on their own some time. Yet
neither of them was willing to take me into their apartment, which they shared with roommates of the opposite
sex. Instead, they gave me the name of a cheap hotel
which they assured me would accept my credit until payday. However, they encouraged me to share my problems with them as much as I desired.

Leaving the office, I decided to explore the possibility
of checking into the hotel my co-workers had suggested.
It was only a few blocks walk from the campus and
seemed my only hope for a haven of refuge in the midst
of a city not known for its kindness to the homeless.

The Paris Hotel was a dive. Blistered paint peeled
from the walls as junkies and prostitutes openly offered
their wares nearby. Sirens pierced the air as police cars
sped off toward crimes committed in the neighboring
tenements. The manager accepted my word that she
would be paid for seven days on Friday, yet a week in
such a place would be too much for me. I purchased a
paper and attempted to find a rooming house able and
willing to take me in.

The Penington was located just a short distance from
the hotel. It was a Quaker-run residence for young
people desiring to make a start in the city. As I walked up
to the iron gates and pressed the bell on one of the two
remaining doors separating the house from the street, I
hoped that I would be accepted more than I had hoped
for anything before in my entire life. A young man
stepped out and ushered me into his office on the first
floor of the five-story walk up building. I liked him immediately.

Dick (whom I did not know was gay until three years

later) took one look at my black eye and seemed concerned. "What can I do for you?" he offered gently. I told him of the dire straits that I was in financially and begged him for a place to stay until payday. I promised him that every penny I owed would be paid in full and suggested that he call my office if he had any further questions or wanted to verify my story. He could feel the desperation in my voice and in a mere moment had planned my future for the coming year.

I would be allowed to stay at the Penington House as long as I liked. Dick was really concerned about me and the plight that I was in. "No problem," he told me. "You've got a home here. Many of the residents are about your age. You needn't fear for anything." Then he added, almost as an afterthought, "I've been through a similar situation in my life. You're going to make it, kid, and I'll help you all I can."

Relaxing for a while after finding relief from the pressure which being homeless had engendered in me, I soon became curious about the house itself, and its members. Venturing into the sitting room, several models ("models to be" I later learned was the proper designation) lounged in front of the television set. A woman with gray hair and a beautiful gold cat smiled warmly. I accepted her smile as an invitation, thus beginning one of the deepest friendships I was to know for years.

Lavinia Lewis was black and beautiful, a teacher in the New York school system, and loved literature. A melancholic lady, she was nevertheless gentle and sensitive. I loved her almost immediately. Lavinia and Edith Darlington, a retired Bell Telephone worker, were the mother and grandmother of the house, respectively.

Each had almost a full-time job relating to all the students and young people who attended New York colleges or trained for various careers while they resided at the house.

Edith was a Quaker. She informed me that the American Friends Service Committee was located next door by the meetinghouse. I was invited to join any of the activities in which this church engaged. I would be a welcome guest at any meeting.

After exploring several relationships with the Quakers who often came to dinner, I did not choose to affiliate with their church. I regarded their meeting as nothing more than a period of meditation. None of the "Friends" I met ever spoke about Jesus, and all were engaged in activities centering around social concerns and political issues. I was not ready for this type of involvement. I had enough trouble at that point getting myself together without trying to keep Africa from starving, or becoming overly concerned about the plight of those less fortunate than myself. Still, one of their activities did interest me. I was able to take part in peace demonstrations for the first time. My involvement in the Army had led me to believe in this as one worthwhile project I could affirm.

As the following year came to a close, and I switched from working at NYU to a job as an occupational therapist's assistant at Beth Israel Medical Center, I became increasingly restless. Something was missing from my life which I couldn't articulate nor define. Once more my thoughts turned to religion.

I had no doubt that I was still a Roman Catholic. After all, I had been raised in the church from my youth. The evangelism of the Jesus People in San Antonio, the prayers of my Seventh-Day Adventist friend, Captain

Johnson, the good work of the Society of Friends politically—none of this had changed my mind on what I believed to be the one true church of Jesus Christ. Guilt overwhelmed me at even the thought of joining another religious group in spite of what had occurred in the monastery. I dismissed such a possible course of action as ridiculous.

Feeling more confident about my future, I was hopeful that something good might come of my life after all. Mulling over my past monastic experiences, I realized that the Second Vatican Council had changed a lot of things in the church. Monastic communities were becoming more humane. Many were actually experiencing a depth of personal relationship and identification with the true needs of a suffering world. What if I chose a small diocesan order somewhere in a rural area. Then I could eliminate the academic rigidity, the large classes, and the medieval lifestyle traditions. Perhaps I could enter an order specifically structured for working with young people. This would add a note of reality and spontaneity to the community. You couldn't be fake for long with kids and they would be an ever-present source of challenge. If only I could find superiors who had their priorities straight, I mused, deciding to approach my priest about the whole thing soon.

My parish, at the time, was located in the heart of Manhattan. My priest was Father O'Meara. I had wandered into the church only a few weeks before, when my desire to return to religious life had become deeper. Through this encounter, I had begun to teach a class on religion and Catholic doctrine to the young people of Puerto Rican descent who comprised the majority of Sunday mass attenders.

Father O'Meara. was kind and understanding, although certainly not one with whom you would discuss a third attempt at monastic living very easily. Being diocesan, he did not have to keep the vows of poverty, chastity, and obedience in the same manner cloistered monks did. In fact, he had not taken the vow of poverty at all. The ordered monks and the diocesan priests had always seen things a little differently in the church, and I wondered what he would say when I confided my desire to try monastic life once again!

Father O'Meara gave me no problems whatsoever. If that was the life I wished to choose, it was my decision to make. Offering the ever-present *Catholic Directory*, he gave me every encouragement. He assured me that the novice masters and postulant masters knew their jobs. I had time to decide what I really wanted. He would help in every way he could, leaving deeper counsel to those who understood more about monastic living than he did.

This final attempt at religious communal living in the Catholic Church began with every effort I could muster to select just the right group. For openers, I discounted every order which had more than one hundred members. Then I found myself considering diocesan communities, groups of monks serving a particular diocese, rather than the international orders of world renown, such as the Franciscans and the Jesuits. Finally, my choice was reduced to two—the Brothers of Saint Pius the Tenth in Oregon or the Brothers of the Holy Rosary in Reno. Both seemed to fit my specifications exactly. I wrote letters and sent them off promptly, while faithfully attending mass and the sacraments until the responses came in.

When the Order of Saint Pius the Tenth had failed to return my inquiry after eight weeks, I discounted it as the place where God might want me to go. Thus my attention focused upon the Brothers of the Most Holy Rosary. I hoped against hope that I would not be rejected out of hand. I dialogued with their superior by mail. The possibility for entrance seemed bright. Further correspondance and a visit from one of their brothers completed the process. I would leave New York and the Quakers, to serve Christ in the Diocese of Reno-Las Vegas, as a Brother of the Holy Rosary. I was ecstatic!

Brothers of the Holy Rosary

Committing one's entire life to a religious order in the Catholic Church is always a frightening venture. Brother Matthew, my new religious superior, met me at the bus station with a warm smile which did much to alleviate my anxiety after traveling three thousand miles to begin a new life among the familiar, but still somehow frightening, monks. A short car ride from downtown Reno, brought us through pasture-lined country roads to the monastery building in Sparks, a little city adjacent to Reno itself. The standard joke was that Reno was so close to hell you could see "sparks." Yet the sheltered existence of the postulant and novice would shield me from the legalized gambling, prostitution, and immorality of the divorce capital of the world for another year and a half.

Once seated in the recreation room with Matthew, I was offered a drink and the answers to my questions of the moment. "Yes," Brother Matthew admitted, "he was young—about twenty-nine." He had been raised in Iowa, and had been in another religious order prior to his present involvement with the Brothers of the Holy Rosary. He would indeed be my novice master and was unsure as to why he had been asked to perform this task by the bishop. Yet, perform it he would with joy. He enjoyed his relationships with Brother David and Brother Robert, he told me, two new entrants that summer. They were good novices and had grown close to the community under his direction. He hoped that our involvement together would prove equally as productive.

I was informed that the main purposes of this order was to facilitate the salvation of each of its members and to assist with the ministry of the church in the Diocese of Reno. This could include various tasks, but generally centered around teaching.

Brother Matthew explained that true holiness consisted of manifesting Christlike character, of being transformed into the same type of person that Jesus was (in His humanity). This would be accomplished by our cooperating with God in the process of sanctification which had begun in our hearts at infant baptism. If we achieved Christlikeness, we would be saved at death, he explained, provided of course that we did not die in mortal (severe) sin. Sanctifying grace seemed to be the answer to holiness. It was given through the sacraments, primarily communion and penance. Maybe this was the key, I thought, to overcoming my propensity for evil, the answer I had been seeking in the Marists and Trinitarians. Since it was the goal of the community to foster in us a desire and ability to use this power to respond back to God out of love, and through our work, perhaps I could make it after all!

Aside from involvement in the sacramental system of the church, by which we would, in Matthews terms, "row upstream against the current of our post-Christian age," we would prove to the sinful world that true Chris-

tianity could be lived even in a city like Reno. We were
to be a light to the world and "way showers" of holiness.

It was Brother Matthew's sincere belief that only work
done out of the true motive of love for God would be acceptable in His sight. As I listened to this intelligent,
zealous, and sincere young monk speak of the ideals of
religious community, my thoughts turned once again to
the words of Thomas Merton: *"Prompter abundantium
divini amoris."* All that you do, everything that you un-
dertake to achieve for Christ must be *"prompter abun-
datium amoris"* (prompted by an overflow of love for
God). I was challenged and truly inspired to become the
best monk at the monastery. I believed that with Matthew's able leadership and his tremendous ability to
relate what I felt was true spirituality, I would find
meaning and peace in my life. Perhaps for the first time
in my life I had found a monk who cared about my soul.
Exhilarated at learning about these keys to holiness, I determined not to fail in this precious opportunity to become the brother I had always hoped to be.

After the traditional confession, mass, and matin
prayers the following morning, I met Brother Robert and
Brother David for the first time. Altogether, six monks
lived at the monastery on Boynton Lane. Matthew and
Ambrose had already taken vows. Brother Damian would
be vowed in a month or two. Thus these three brothers
would recreate separately and we would not be allowed
to fellowship with them in any way. However, Brother
Robert and Brother David had entered the house only a
few months before me. Thus I would, in a sense, become
a part of their novice class, even as they recreated with
me, the only postulant.

Brother Robert was from Johnstown, Pennsylvania. He

was seventeen, and had practically been raised by the nuns. Graduating from Catholic elementary school, he proceeded on to local parochial high school, where he became the president of his class. He had an ardent devotion to Mary and his room was transformed into a shrine for her. Later he was to teach his class of fifth-grade students at Holy Cross all about how the Archangel Michael had transported the Blessed Virgin to heaven bodily as Michael the Archangel's purple wings enfolded her, making her trip to the celestial city (the Assumption) a most thrilling event, at least to his students.

Brother David was a scrawny young man who always looked hungry. He was nervous and smoked on occasion when tension arose. A naturally conciliatory nature, sensitivity, and an above-average intelligence characterized his personality. Yet both he and Robert never really seemed to like me much. David often withdrew from my presence when hassles arose and Robert simply retreated to his shrine whenever the going got rough.

My responsibility at the monastery, with the help of the other novices, was to keep both the mansion itself and its adjoining property neat and clean. As the old Flick estate included thirty bedrooms, a large livingroom, a chapel, and a kitchen, this was no easy task. While I never joyed prolonged periods of housecleaning and gardening, it seemed that some exercise or class would always rise just when I became bored beyond hope.

Perhaps the most distinctive tradition of the order was the daily recitation of the Rosary. This occurred at 5:00 each afternoon. Although I was unfamiliar with biblical injunctions against vain repetitions, I still found this practice most distasteful. Brother Matthew described the purpose of this constant repetition of the Hail Mary as much like the use of a mantra in Eastern religion. Its purpose, he said, was to clear the mind of distraction so that we could meditate on the various important incidents of Christ's life more easily. Still, I was confused. How could one pray,

> Hail Mary, full of grace, the Lord is with you. Blessed are you among women and blessed is the fruit of your womb, Jesus. Holy Mary, mother of God, pray for us sinners, now and at the hour of our death. Amen.

fifty times, without concentrating on the words themselves. To justify the practice one had to use the prayer as a mantra indeed, concentrating on the "mysteries" of the Lord's earthly life. Yet it always seemed to me that this split one's attention unrealistically. If I was praying to Mary, didn't she want my full attention? How could I give it to her when my mind was not supposed to be focused on the words I was praying?

Moral and dogmatic theology classes were given by eminent priests of the diocese, one of whom is now a Bishop in Oregon. These men held responsible positions in the hierarchy of the church. They had each received training in Rome and were canon lawyers. Their presence in our midst was always treated with gravity and humble submission.

One day, while I hotly debated a point of theology, a question arose about the impact of the brothers on the larger community of Reno. My perception was that there didn't appear to have been much. At this juncture, Father Rhigini, the highly respected Chancellor of the Diocese (who has since been elevated to Monsignor), substantiated my argument by saying of the brothers, "Never has so much been given to so many that produced so little." Brother David and Brother Robert were horrified, and Brother Matthew called me into his office for a severe reprimand. Clearly, honesty in intellectual pursuit and practical self-evaluation were not applauded. Yet, aside from this, the philosophy and dogma we learned in those classes were a constant challenge to my academic interests.

Toward the end of my postulancy of six months, I was approved by the Brothers' Council to receive the habit of the order and a new name. This was mandatory. I was told to submit three choices of names to the superior, who would convey them to the bishop. He would announce my new name at the ceremony which was to take place under his personal ministry a few weeks later. I selected Keith, Shawn, and Kevin as names to symbolize my death to the old man of the secular world and birth to the new man I would supposedly become by acceptance into the religious community.

Dawn had only broken a few hours earlier as I was escorted into the little chapel for the ceremony of investiture. Golden rays of light were filtered into purple haze by the stained-glass windows. This seemed to add an element of penance for past sin to the symbolism of the service. Kneeling on the front steps of the altar at the feet of the bishop, my black coat and tie were taken from me. In their place I was helped into the long floor-length white robe unique to this community. A wide black sash served as a belt and sandals were optional, but I chose to wear them as symbolic of humility and poverty. Finally, an ebony crucifix was placed around my neck. These were the proud emblems of my acceptance by the Roman Catholic Church as a novice in religious life, which I had won through completion of my training and affirmation of the brotherhood. My hopes soared as the bishop pronounced the solemn words for all to hear: "In the world you were known as George William Linehan. Henceforth, you will be known as Brother Kevin." My heart pounded away in my chest permeated with the realization of dreams I had come to doubt would ever be fulfilled.

A solemn mass began, with all the mysterious awe that always seemed present when celebrated by a bishop or a cardinal. Matthew, my novice master, smiled at me from his choir stall. I had been accepted! I was loved! I was a monk after all!

As the following year of novitiate training wore on, we were invited to visit the Brothers' House in Las Vegas, about 500 miles away for a week. Once there, I cleaned, cooked, and assisted the monks in whatever way I could, meeting Phillip and several other members of the community for the first and only prolonged period.

Aside from this vacation away from the monastery in Sparks, we were allowed little freedom. All of us had the same schedule. My mail was read before I received it, and outgoing correspondence was always perused by Brother Matthew as well. We were never permitted to stay outside of the house overnight. When we were away for any length of time at all, whether to attend a class at the university or to teach at the Catholic grade school, we were always in "twos" and were escorted in the communal car. I never established a single personal relationship with anyone outside the monastery during the entire year I spent there. All my money was kept in an account in my name by the superior. Apart from one or two carefully planned visits to Reno stores, always accompanied by Brother Matthew, I did not become acquainted with the physical layout of the city of Reno at all.

My novitiate was finally coming to a close! I was elated. Having passed the requirements for entrance into the novice class the year before, I had every hope that I would also pass the next milestone successfully. True, Brother David and Brother Robert had begun avoiding me (and me them) lately. "Irresolvable personality clashes," as Matthew phrased it, had developed between us in the course of our training. Still this was hardly surprising when three men had only each other with whom to communicate for over a year!

The rigid structure of the formulation program was at an end. With a more relaxed and congenial atmosphere created by our all being accepted into the order for vows, there was hope for reconciliation in the future. Perhaps Matthew, Damian, and Ambrose would be able to help us iron out our differences when we were free to fellowship with them as well as one another. We all recognized that we were living under an artificial and overly rigorous training period which Vatican II would correct in the near future, we hoped. No, there was nothing to worry about. I could look forward to vows with joy and peace.

It was 4:30 p.m. on a Thursday afternoon when I received the call to come to Brother Matthew's office at once! My mind was in no way prepared for what was to occurr in those next few minutes! Opening the door to Matthew's office, I saw him with tear-stained eyes seated stiffly at his desk. I was horrified. This was not his style. He had only cried one time during the period I had known him. Whatever produced the tears of this normally unemotional and highly self-controlled monk should surely be avoided like the plague, but what was it?

Motioning me to be seated, Brother Matthew began slowly and almost in a whisper. "The brothers . . ." He stopped, gained control, and began once again, "The brothers held chapter this morning." He looked away from me out the window to his right. "They denied your petition for vows. Please lay your habit on the chair and leave the monastery as soon as possible." Those "personality clashes" with Brother Robert and Brother David had been taken as an indication that I was not fit to join the community after all.

Once more I experienced the injustices of Catholic religious life. My entire future lay in the hands of the monks at that chapter meeting! Aside from Matthew and Ambrose, none of the others who voted had more than a passing acquaintance with me while I was a guest at their monastery in Las Vegas. Matthew mentioned that they may have heard things from others (Robert and David?) which was not in my favor. I was given no opportunity whatsoever to defend myself. There was no exhortation to repent and no meeting with the brothers face-to-face to attempt reconciliation or receive exhortation in areas where I was deficient. Matthew was not skilled in "group dynamics," as he called it. He had spoken with me about the poor quality of my relationships with Robert and David in the past. This should have solved the problem. It had not. I would leave at once.

Rejection, long my faithful friend, kissed me once again, and I knew that this time we were to be companions for a long time.

One Thousand Dollars for a Grief-Filled Week

When I stopped letting myself think or feel, switching to automatic, I do not exactly recall. Perhaps it was at the moment I heard the word "leave." I was in a state of complete emotional shock, not really too much aware of what was really happening on a conscious level. In such situations, I did not usually function well. For some reason the thought of going to college fastened itself in my mind.

Matthew agreed to let me stay overnight at the monastery until I could catch a plane to New York the next morning. Why I associated New York with college, I'll never know. Perhaps it was because I had worked at New York University. In any case, as the first rays of sunlight illumined the always snow-capped mountains near Reno, about thirteen hours after my dismissal, I was on a jet heading back to the Penington House and the Quakers.

Once home again, I applied for admission to NYU. Acceptance was no difficulty whatsoever. However, upon receiving admission to the college I realized my dwindling finances would not cover the first semester's tuition. The flight had cost $325. I had $675 left from the resources on account with the superior when I left the brothers. I could count on some assistance from the "G.I. Bill," but the costs at such an expensive university would be much more than this. When I explained my dilemma to Lavinia, she suggested that I should return to Nevada. I would be able to attend the less expensive state college there, as my residence in the monastery had qualified me for in-state tuition. Thus only a few days after arriving in the city I once again boarded a plane, returning to Reno. Another $325, which I paid for this ticket left me close to broke and I still had no place to live.

After deplaning at the Reno Airport, every emotion I had been suppressing for days overwhelmed me like a tidal wave. I had no acquaintance with the town and felt totally helpless, rejected, lost, alone, frightened, and miserable. Setting my suitcase down on the marble floor, oblivious to everyone around, I simply started to cry.

In a few moments, the ticket clerk for one of the airlines bent down and inquired gently, "Where are you headed for, friend?"

Unable to find many words, I simply replied, almost in a whisper, "I wish I knew."

With compassion the clerk continued his empathetic inquiry, "Got no ideas at all?"

I weakly explained my somewhat nebulous hope to attend the university.

"Look, why don't you take a cab up toward the U," he ventured. "You may get some help up there."

I nodded slowly and rose. Picking up my luggage once again, I hailed a taxi, informing the driver of my general destination. She asked me for a specific address. I halted. There was none to give her. "Oh, just anywhere up by the college," I suggested. Observing my tear-stained eyes, mussed hair, and depressed demeanor, the driver asked no more questions and headed off in what seemed a generally western direction.

Leaving the taxi, I paid the fare and sat down on the curb to plan my next move. I couldn't do it. I didn't have the strength of will even to try. I wanted nothing more than to die right there. Yet I knew that the police would become suspicious of my prolonged presence on the corner and decided to head for a motel I could see two blocks away. Once registered and showered, I determined to find the admissions office and inquire about admittance and costs for the coming term.

The registrar seemed to me like a cross between Father

Lupo and my ex-drill instructor, as I explained my desire to seek admission as a full-time student for the fall term. High school transcripts, V.A. eligibility certificates, and other documents must all be ordered immediately. I should not have applied so late. There was little time to complete the necessary forms. On and on he droned, making demands left and right. "No," he finally stated in answer to my one paramount question of the moment, "no dorm space is available until you are officially accepted. And even if you are, you can't move in until the first week of September."

Feeling myself starting to lose control of my emotions, I quickly completed the last form and shuffled dejected away from the office. Only two hundred dollars of my savings was left in my pocket, and that wouldn't last long in a motel which charged ten dollars a night. What was I going to do until school began (if I was accepted at that).

Three blocks from the registrar's office I felt unable to keep myself together emotionally any longer. Spying a beautiful white building, I entered and sat down on a newly upholstered chair. Tears burst from the depths of my heavy-laden heart once more. I swayed back and forth in the chair slowly, trying to convince myself that everything was going to be all right.

Just then, the director of the building came over and asked me why I was crying in his lobby. I explained that I was an ex-monk in a strange city and pretty well overcome by everything I had been through in the past week. Needing and receiving a sympathetic ear from this gentleman, I ventured further. I told him that I had no where to live until classes started in several weeks and had only two hundred dollars with which to support myself during that time.

Much to my surprise, Mr. Brown, my newfound friend, told me that I had stumbled into a private, seven-story housing development for collegians! He was in charge of assisting students who wished to live there. The fact that I was not as yet officially accepted did not disqualify me from consideration of his services. He even agreed to rent me a room for the sum I had left until classes began in the fall and stated cheerfully that meals would be included!

Signing a contract on the spot, I became a permanent resident of the College Inn. Once again I had a "home." I was no longer without some direction in my life. Perhaps, I thought, if the university couldn't give me a better understanding of God, it could at least teach me a marketable skill. I'd try my best to equip myself for some occupation. There must be some profession other than monastery life for me in the world and I would have four long years to find it.

Undergraduate Games

Playboy Magazine once named the University of Nevada at Reno as one of the top ten party schools in the nation. With this assessment I heartily agree. Although my first two years as an undergraduate netted me a 3.5 GPA and a certain degree of ability to relate with my fellow students on an academic level, surpassing that which I had previously known, I was forced to concede that most of my colleagues in class were more concerned about social activities than they were about pursuing serious intellectual inquiry.

Drugs, sex, and alcohol seemed the primary pursuits. Students were either cruising for these commodities or enjoying them already, having obtained them for the day, the weekend, or the semester. A standard joke became that the third floor of the College Inn was so high it floated over the seventh! The GTOs, XKEs, and Jaguars parked in the communal garage gave ample evidence that one's hopes of enjoying college life were better realized when material wealth enhanced popularity won either on the ski slopes or at "the party"!

Morality was definitely situational. The pervading philosophy was liberal, existential, and certainly non-Christian. Campus policy was permissive so long as one "maintained" his studies and was discreet. Few, if any, administrators seemed to care about what went on behind closed doors so long as no one got hurt. "Hurt" appeared to imply either serious physical injury, flipping out over drugs, or becoming pregnant.

The goal of most of the students in my class concerning their college careers seemed to be, "Get that piece of paper with as little personal effort as possible." By "piece of paper" they meant their Bachelor's Degree. Without it, they said, one was fated to live a professional life of low pay and little real responsibility. Thus it must be obtained. But there were ways to make the experience almost painless. The trick was to find them.

Public universities always attempt to delineate clearly between matters of church and matters of state. Thus no truth, except that canonized by scientific or empirical study, is officially taught as objectively valid. This left us with a tremendous wealth of more or less factual data taught from virtually no concrete perspective whatsoever. How we related the myriad of facts spewed forth from professors into our lecture notebooks was purely a matter of personal choice. The responsibility for effectual absorption and integration was ours alone.

Realizing that my nominal Catholicism, sporadic attendance at mass, and rapidly crumbling head knowledge of Christianity were doomed to die an imminent death in this environment anyway, I determined to approach my problem head on. Systematically I reviewed my faith in Christ and the Roman Catholic Church. There was no substance to it any longer (if there ever had been). Christ was, in reality, simply a hope I held out to myself. The church was nothing more than a constant source of pain and rejection. It was a huge, monolithic, and bureaucratic structure in which I felt myself a total stranger fleeing from it's authoritarian and unnervingly irrelevant demands.

No longer could I conjure up within myself a faith in grace being channeled through the sacraments. While prayer might hold some validity, nothing was really changed by it. My religion was totally dead. I could not, I admitted, consistently manifest good works. Perhaps I had been deluding myself, holding onto Catholicism out of prior programming and culturally engendered guilt, afraid at the prospect of exploring the many new ideas clamoring for attention on campus.

In the final analysis, a gut-level recognition crept over me. College had not destroyed my faith. It simply exposed the now inescapable fact that I never had any! What I previously identified as faith was hope—hope pure and simple, hope that in the end Jesus might really turn out to be what parents, priests, and even some peers had said He was, yet what I myself did not know Him to be.

Added to this spiritual dilemma came an unmistakably relevant insight. If Jesus was really who so many had claimed to believe He was in the Catholic Church, why did people take that fact so glibly? Few Catholics with whom I had ever spoken—including my parents, religious superiors, and fellow monks—ever actually spoke much about "the Lord Jesus" personally. Rather, morality seemed always the underlying objective of their indirect referances to Him. Could it be that Jesus, Catholicism, and religious (or moral) living were nothing but what Lenin had claimed that they were—an opiate for the people to keep them in check, a sort of protection against anarchy perpetuated for the sake of someone's determination of the "common good"? I simply did not know.

Intellectual integrity was a concept that I determined to accept. Not knowing the meaning of truth had to be admitted. In all honesty, I must acknowledge what I did not possess in order to arrive at that which I sought. No longer would I pretend to be something that I was not. No longer would I sit in the chair of the deists and theists at the college. No longer would I defend any idea in which I did not wholeheartedly believe. One thing I definitely did not believe now was that Christianity was any better than any other religion, philosophy, or ideal.

Coming Out

During my second year of undergraduate work for the degree in speech communications I had decided to obtain, I moved away from the College Inn. Sharing a room with a guy who was involved in constant sexual exploits with female lovers, often when I was also present, had become too much for me. I rented a small apartment, really half a basement, from an alcoholic lady about three blocks from the college and moved in. I considered this the first real home of my own.

The freedom of living alone really appealed to me. No one cared when I came and went, and I always had a place of refuge where I could flee when personal problems arose. I discovered another "advantage" in this move to apartment dwelling. Two female students living in the other half of the basement which I had rented became constant companions, and Judy and Gerry were the first two persons with whom I could be totally honest about my homosexuality.

"Coming out," or informing others of one's gayness, is never an easy task. Not one time in my entire life had I shared the fact that I was not heterosexual with anyone. Lies were prompted by fear whenever people inquired about my sexual preference. I could not risk losing the professional benefits of my hard won degree. Who knew what might happen if the label "gay" was ever attached to me!

Gerry was the one who opened the door of my closet with her classical candor. She had undergone two abortions during the period I knew her. Gerry was intelligent, perceptive, totally self-confident, and sex was one of her favorite pastimes. Gerry deeply enjoyed her affairs. She seemed to believe that those who either said they didn't have any affairs or didn't enjoy sexual encounters when they did occur, were lying or sick. If heterosexual encounters were so enjoyable to her even outside of marriage, I thought, perhaps my past suicide attempt was precipitated more by guilt and the wrong partner than by any actual inherent sinfulness in the homosexual act.

Judy and Gerry discussed my sexuality at length, in the way that only two college girls could do. Gerry, especially, encouraged me to find "just the right person," limiting my sexual experiences always to those whom I really loved (whatever that meant). I should seek a lover who was himself searching for a lifelong relationship. There were many gays on campus, Gerry assured me, who were just as lonely and miserable as I was. "Get out there and live," she told me. "Don't be afraid. These are modern times. Shed your chains"—these were her constant admonitions.

Shortly after an especially long conversation with the girls one afternoon, I decided to take a walk to mull over their advice. I slowly sauntered along the road in the deepening twilight. There always seemed to be something magical about evening, that period between total light and total darkness. I felt one with my world. The stars were beginning to appear, and over the roof of a nearby car, I saw a satellite winding its way through the path of the stars like a free spirit observing the world with a smile.

"Hello there," he offered almost in a whisper. Looking down, only a few feet lower than the path of the now rapidly disappearing stellar communications device, I saw him sitting casually on the hood of a Ford. *My God*, I gasped, *he's beautiful. Are you sure you're not dreaming?*

Murl grinned broadly. His sky-blue eyes, square and masculine jaw, sandy hair, and well-proportioned body became more visible as I approached him, almost afraid to believe what was happening. "Hi, man, what's happening?" I replied, drawing closer to him as my nervousness increased. "Oh, let him be gay," I prayed to myself. "Please, God, let him be gay," I repeated.

"Nothing much," he said. "I'm just sort of sitting here looking for someone to talk to. The guys back at the fraternity house are getting drunk again, and I thought

I'd better leave while the getting was good." Murl pointed in the general direction of the Phi Sig House next door.

It was now or never I decided. "Listen, man, why not come home to my house and have some dinner with me. I only live on the next street," I stated pointing toward the apartment. "It won't take long." There was no doubt about it, I joyfully thought as Murl joined me a moment later. I've finally hit the jackpot. He was gay indeed!

Yes, it was a dream come true! Murl and I enjoyed a total relationship that seemed completely fulfilling. He was intelligent, sensitive, and gentle. My hopes now centered on remaining his for life. None of the attraction I felt toward this beautiful man was based on a desire for sexual involvement per se, although sex was one aspect of our more (much more) encompassing relationship. Rather, I loved Murl for all that he was as a person. It was my sincere conviction that sex apart from love was destructive, violent, and ultimately extremely damaging, but I was in love with Murl.

I could honestly say that Murl and I were deeply responsive to one another's needs for acceptance, affirmation, and intimacy. We were respectful of each other's dreams, hopes, and aspirations. This constituted a new dimension of living which I had never known before. Rather than condemning me for my lack of holiness or morality, or my failure to meet society's expectations for me, Murl offered himself to me just as he was, just as I was. I couldn't help but rejoice in the reverie of a relationship in which whatever little I had to offer another person was received with gratitude, understanding, and even delight.

All my prior life had been a vain attempt to live the

Law. My need for love seemed to be totally eclipsed by its demands. I was starving for affection, and I knew that Murl was too. If Law and love—God's command against homosexuality and my need for a gay relationship—conflicted, to hell with the Law. In the final analysis what good was a man's slavish obedience to divine decrees apart from love? No, I would place myself squarely in opposition to all that militated against my new lifestyle. Who knew, I wondered during those days, that God even existed anyway?

Another factor which compelled me to continue affirming my relationship with Murl was the belief that honesty demanded it. To deny my homosexuality seemed the height of hypocrisy. If there was a God, He certainly would include honesty amid His other myriad of demands upon me. How could I honestly ever say that I was not gay. Homosexuality was not something you did; it was something you were. For God to condemn gayness would be for Him to condemn me. Thus I felt doomed to hell anyway I looked at it. Why not enjoy whatever happiness I could find, before death either annihilated me totally or God condemned me ultimately (if He existed at all).

Perhaps the most enjoyable times of our relationship were the days that Murl and I visited the car museum, went swimming together in a desert lake, romped through the wilderness of the Sierra Nevadas, and simply basked in the love we saw in each other's eyes as we walked together in the rain.

Contentment permeated my being as I saw him asleep beside me in the morning with sunlight streaming through the window, scattered in a million directions by his golden hair. Then I was free to touch those deep angular cheek bones, the hair on his arms, and admire his white teeth so often set off from his tan face by his smiling lips. I rejoiced to know that he was here, beside me, because this was where he chose to be, because it was comfortable, secure, and where he belonged by the rights of love. The thrill of this aspect of our relationship meant more to me than any orgasm ever did.

Still, there was sexual pleasure. Nighttime, once that long, dark, lonely burden of each twenty-four hours, was transformed into a garden of delight. To have him so close, to hold and caress him while being held by him, to give and receive, sharing our very bodies together, was all that life need ever offer me for me to embrace its promise, believe its worth, express its meaning.

Never had anyone told me that homosexuality could be so fulfilling. Why, I wondered throughout those idyllic days, did anyone condemn the practice? Only since learning to love Murl did life appear truly a friend, not an enemy. Those whose todays were rough and ragged were the ones who lived in a dream world of future goals and expectations. I was certainly no longer among them!

One afternoon shortly after Murl had left for class, I called Mom and Dad. They had to be the first to know. Sure, they wouldn't approve at first. Yet they were still my family. Who knew? Maybe they would accept my relationship with Murl in time.

The phone rang. A voice answered. It was Mother. Some small talk convinced me she was in a good mood. I could feel my stomach muscles tighten with nervousness. Summing up all my courage the news spilled forth from me through the phone as important to my mind as the shot heard round the world. I was going to ask Murl to marry me. I had found love at last. Though it was not the heterosexual kind most people enjoy, I had no doubt that it was real, deep, and lasting.

Silence filled the apartment, a silence so awesome it filled every crack and corner of the basement, deafening me with rejection, hostility, and fear. Finally, in an eternal moment, it was over. Mother's voice crackled with harshness and conviction. "Every time I see your face I will vomit," she said, then hung up without another word. Placing the phone down on the receiver I retreated to the couch to think, yet hopefully not to feel.

Murl smiled his usual gentle smile as he opened the door. He had forgotten a needed textbook. My tears could not be hidden. Hugging and holding me in the security of his massive arms, he seemed to encapsulate every hope for love I would ever have. There was absolutely no way I could ever leave him, even if I wanted to. I was possessed by his love. Stroking my mussed hair from my tear-stained face, he whispered softly, "The parents?" I nodded, burying my face in his chest, sobbing uncontrollably as we rocked back and forth in a deep embrace. Then hell began.

After confiding to Murl the reason for the phone call I expected him to be as elated as I. Yet such was not the case. "You shouldn't have done it, kid," he said. "You shouldn't have done it. I can't make it with just you for a lifetime. I can't promise you that kind of relationship. All I can give you is today. Who knows what will happen tomorrow?"

I bolted in disbelief. *Why, why,* I thought to myself, *it was sure. I mean, didn't we love each other? Wasn't the future ours? Wouldn't we make it together?*

Murl's deep blue eyes grew almost black. I knew no

sun would follow the storm which raged in his heart. No further explanations were necessary. No begging would help. I quoted him a line from our favorite song: "So if today is our last one, let's run out into the sun." Linda Ronstad's lyrics struck home. That afternoon was all the future I had strength to think about and far too soon, for me, it was over.

Only two months after my phone conversation with Mother, he left. Although he had come into my life in an incredible manner, actually calling me to him in a chance meeting on the street, I always loved him. There was never to be another Murl for me in college. I made one attempt after another in a futile effort to find the phamtom I now harbored in my heart, my dreams, my mind. Caustically, this ever present spirit, this ghost, this new Murl who always eluded me, I dubbed "Mr. Right." Cruising, I searched for him on the street, coyly I bartered for him in class, casually I bumped into him here or there, but always he fled away, disappearing into a thousand situations and circumstances beyond my control.

Instead of Murl I married a partner not of my own choosing. His name was loneliness. I came to know him better than I had ever dared to hope to know Murl. He followed me everywhere. Never would he leave me. Always we walked arm and arm. Sometimes we fought. Sometimes I thought we would separate. Sometimes I tried to kill him for the anguish his presence entailed. But never, from the time I saw my ex-lover leave, did loneliness ever depart. I came to understand an old saying but to interpret my way. I knew with no doubt at all that it was not better to have loved and lost than not to have loved at all.

More Study Out of Class Than In

If they gave degrees for self-study, instead of credits completed, I should have mine by now, I mused, settling in for another long session of exploring philosophy. Ayn Rand was my goddess of the moment. Howard Roark, her hero in the *Fountainhead*, was my man of the hour. It was the fall of my sophomore year. Inhaling every word of her writings, I believed that Ms. Rand was a woman to be heard. Her concept of enlightened self-interest was based squarely on empiricism. Altruism had become my enemy. After reading *Atlas Shrugged, The Fountainhead, For the New Intellectual, Anthem,* and others, the programming was almost complete.

From Ms. Rand's work I established some basic tenets of faith which I held as inviolable. Several of them were presuppositions which I developed as guideposts for my life.

Presupposition 1: There is no God beside myself.

Presupposition 2: Man has a logical rational mind, and has the inherent ability to think logically.

Presupposition 3: Empiricism is the only valid method for making logical decisions.

Rule 1: Allow the creativity inherent in your own being free expression.

Rule 2: Your only integration point is yourself.

Rule 3: Others exist but they are secondary. They should never be allowed to interfere with the free expression of one's own thoughts and ideas.

Rule 4: Develop your inherent ability to think logically and never let emotional considerations dissuade you from your purposes.

Rule 5: You are only worth the ideas you have plus your willingness to put those ideas into effect by struggle and perseverance.

Rule 6: Suffering born out of self-expression is to be disregarded. Take no notice of it. It might hinder your efforts.

Yes, Rand's meaning was clear. I lived to serve myself, to express myself, to be myself. I regarded others as mere bystanders on the road of life, of value only in what they had to offer me in the fulfillment of my own purposes. No amount of effort, no degree of study, no demand of project or performance would deter me. Rather, I would embrace them in pursuit of my ideas and goals.

Integrity, being true to oneself, this was the key. The enemy was the mediocre man, the second-hander, the society ruling through committee and conclave who did not understand me-Prometheus yet unchained, the man with an idea he would die for. Tradition and the system, religion and the state, always attempted to sap me of my fulfillment in the past, to convince me that I was not my own integration point. No longer would I allow these influences to shackle me.

Now I was alive, now I knew my real purpose. For the first time since picking up *Anthem*, Rand's entire thesis became clear that fall. She didn't want me to become a slave to her. She didn't want to be my god. No, rather her message was that of a prophet, a way-shower, as well as a fellow pilgrim in the world. Her works pointed me, not toward following her, but to following my own creativity and individuality—wherever that would lead.

And the Walls Came Tumbling Down

History class was in progress as I seated myself in the last chair toward the door that spring of my sophomore year. Professor Houghton was philosophizing again.

Paradigms and examples of man's past failure to create a humane world all gave rise to his theory of historical interpretation. Reaching the climax of his "sermon," he almost shouted at the students. "Therefore, we learn one great fact from history: men do not learn from history. They are irrational creatures who, although they should integrate principles from past experiences, seldom do."

Irrational, I thought. Not learning from past failures, I mused. Well, he's "off the wall," I concluded. Man was rational and logical. That he seldom used his ability to think rationally, even if conceded, did not mean that he did not retain the capacity within him to do so . . . or did it? Why did man so seldom think logically? Why was history filled with awful atrocities unexplainable to the rational mind? Why had emotional and cultural influences so often overwhelmed him? Could it be that man's ability to think logically was limited? Perhaps he was unable to utilize his innate resources for some reason. History seemed filled with evidence that something had happened to man some place way back in the dim past of his evolutionary development limiting his potential. I decided to discuss it with the prof but first I would test the waters with the few questions.

My initial inquiry was succinct and to the point. "Dr. Houghton, have you ever read any of the work of Ayn Rand, and if so what did you think of her philosophy?"

Happy about my interest in his prior lecture, the instructor asked me a question in return. "Do you think that man really thought logically, and if so was his thinking really based on empirical evidence?" Then he added, "If you believe man was logical and did base his thinking on empirical evidence, what standard do you use to judge empiricism worthy of such a high priority in your thinking as a method of approach?"

Walking alone now down the long hallway in the growing twilight of the spring afternoon, I was perplexed. Eric Fromm's paradoxical relativism expressed in *The Art of Loving* came vividly to mind. In that book, Fromm had attempted to destroy Western man's rationale for accepting Aristotelian logic, presenting it as somewhat inadequate. Yet, the law of contradiction (that A cannot be both A and non-A) seemed to be the foundation of logical thinking. I moved on in my mind, recognizing now the truth of Kant in his *Critique of Pure Reason*. All logic was indeed based on one's faith in primary presuppositions. Who knew that mine were objectively valid. Empiricism seemed to limit my presuppositions by denying that which could be validated by the five senses.

Filled with the frustration of these new thoughts, I wandered into Dr. Rosenburg's office in the Art Department. Sharing my philosophical dilemma with him simply brought a shrug of his shoulders. The ready smile and elfish twitch of moustache which accompanied his jokes in class were gone. "You know, kid, you think too much. I don't know the answers. What do you need, a physician, a philosopher, or a priest?"

Embarrassed over being treated as if I were some sort of weirdo, and realizing that little help would be forthcoming from him, I simply slunk away into the hall, mumbling an "I don't know, Dr. Rosenburg. I just don't know what I need."

Back home in my apartment that evening I summed up my dilemma in the following question. Can truth be known, and if so can I know it really, personally, and experientially? I had to admit that logic seemed an able method of philsophical thought, and one had to start somewhere. Descartes had begun with himself. "I think, therefore I am." But even this was based on a logical evaluation of his condition. What would a paradoxical relativist like Fromm do with Descartes' perception? According to Fromm, and in line with Eastern thought, Descartes might have thought and not thought at the same time! Therefore he may have been and not been at the same time! Thus all Descartes' further deductions would be both true and false, at least potentially.

Still, there seemed to be that kernel of insight in Kant's *Critique*. All logical reasoning is based on faith. Faith, I thought. Kant sure seemed right. Whether a paradoxical relativist or an Aristotelian logician, one had to have some sort of faith that you were in the right system. No matter where you looked, even in the area of abstract philosophy as a discipline, faith loomed up to stare you in the face. Even rational thinking was based on some form of that commodity which had always eluded me.

Even after hours of careful contemplation, I did not know how to resolve my dilemma. Eastern thinking, that of Fromm, seemed to become as justifiable as Western thinking, that of Aristotle. Empiricism began to look confining. What possible things were objectively there that we were not able to quantify? How could I, who had no faith in God, place any faith in the philosophy of men?

By the time dawn had broken I was still considering the works of great philosophers I had read. Camus had won a Pulitzer Prize for *The Stranger* and seemed a brilliant thinker. I couldn't get over his assessment of man's condition in *Caligula, The Myth of Sisyphus,* and *The Plague*. To him everything was summed up in one word "absurd." He couldn't seem to come to grips with the faith problem himself. Nietzsche, writing in *The Birth of Tragedy and the Genealogy of Morals*, as well as in *Man and Superman*, seemed to place his faith in himself or in man's evolutionary development. Other students on campus generally held the view that the object of one's faith was irrelevant. Most of them saw faith pragmatically, not so much in terms of its object but some form of *ex opere operato* quality which integrated men into happier, better functioning beings.

Yet, to me, there seemed to be a problem, no matter what road you chose. Faith seemed only as valid as the object of one's faith. If I was to place my faith in myself and I failed, what good would that have been? If my faith was placed in mankind at large, and they destroyed themselves in a nuclear holocaust, what value would my faith have had then? If I placed my faith in any philosophical system and it proved wrong, what would my life have proven?

The only valid place to rest faith appeared to be in truth. But what if empiricism was not a sufficient basis for establishing truth? What if there was a truth you could not see, feel, touch, or objectively validate by limitations in scientific methods? How did you know what form of thinking brought truth? It all seemed to rest on faith. But I didn't have any.

Kierkegaard and Teilhard de Chardin seemed to posit one possible answer to my faith crisis. In their writings they seemed to speak about a leap of faith. Yet this appeared to me at the time to be more like the hope I had nursed concerning God while in the Catholic Church years ago. It just didn't seem to be a real faith at all. What if I lept to the wrong object of faith? How did

those who made a leap know that they were on solid foot-
ing once they landed? No, such an approach appeared
somehow contradictory by definition.

Okay, I know what I'll do, I finally decided. Rushing
out of my apartment, I headed for the home of my
professor of comparative religions. Dr. Rants was the first
woman graduate of the Union at Berkeley. While a
student there she had majored in philosophical theology.
Maybe she would have an answer. If she did not, I would
somehow use whatever response she could give me as a
compass bearing. I would search her words out carefully.
Understanding both philosophy and theology, she would
be the best point of reference I now possessed.

I felt no apprehension about ringing her doorbell at an
early hour of the morning, nor did I question her willingness to speak with me. She had consistently given me As
in her classes and, I had reason to believe, considered me
one of her finest students. In a few moments I was sitting
at the kitchen table while a fresh pot of strong black coffee purred away on the stove. In bedroom slippers and
nightgown, this patient young professor smiled at me
and encouraged me to tell her all about the problems I
brought with me.

With sympathetic gentleness, this sensitive prof accepted the seriousness of my problem. She recognized
that I had been shaken to the foundation of my thinking.
What I used as a guideline for thought determined my
actions. This crisis was very real and very deep. She did
not seem to feel herself to be wasting her time in giving
me a heartfelt reply. The only problem was, she didn't
have one.

"Truth is subjective and relative," she explained.
"Each person has to find truth for himself. I would not

presume to interfere with your search for meaning and purpose in life. Perhaps you will ultimately find that life holds, not one truth or meaning or purpose for you, but many!"

Dejectedly, I offered one final inquiry. "What justifies a person's going on in life without truth?" (Or, in her terms, "truth for him"?)

Her answer stopped me cold. "Hope," she replied. "Go on in the hope that one day you will find your truth."

I simply could not believe what I was hearing. Hope had been my motivation for many years spent in monastic living. It had precipitated my entrance into the university. That was no answer. A person had to go on more than hope. I recalled a poem by a black poet I had read some time before. "What happens to hope deferred?" In Harlem it had led to the breaking of many men's spirits. I was absolutely nowhere and I knew it. Philosophical inquiry had netted me precisely nothing in terms of truth. My only path now seemed to be in experience. Perhaps there truth might somehow loom up at me one day when I least expected it. That is, if it did so soon. I knew with certainty I did not wish to verbalize that a man cannot live long with hope as fragile as mine!

Anything Goes!

My early morning interview with Dr. Rants brought my literary search for truth to an abrupt halt. From that time on, I became convinced that the truth must be found in the course of life's experiences. Books simply presented various author's interpretations of it. Who knew which of them was right?

Yes, the key seemed to be in accumulating experience.

Perhaps this alone would open the door to knowledge and certainty, to right and wrong, to the true and to the false. Yet, how long I could maintain myself without the truth bred of experience I did not know.

As the spring semester of my junior year rapidly neared completion, I began to relate as deeply as I could to the few friends that I had kept during my Randian period. Each of them appeared to have something to offer me that had not previously been a part of my life. Involvement in anything that came my way through them might precipitate some sort of discovery of new insight paving the road toward experiencing truth, I thought.

Susan was about thirty-five. We shared advanced classes in medieval literature. She was an avid Theosophist and tipped tables, attended seance sessions, and inquired of Ouija boards. My one big session at the Edgar Cayce Church to which she dragged me netted the confidence of a medium in deep trance that I had a Bodhisatva ("Guide") who was a dead lama, and that I would attain Nirvana in this life time, thus ending my repeated incarnations. That seemed fine to me. I held Tibetan lamas in high esteem (dead or alive) and it gave me security to know that perhaps, indeed, there were guiding forces over me who were treating me well.

Comparative religion classes indicated that Sue must be right about prophets. We read long passages from Dr. Bucke's *Cosmic Consciousness* which indicated that all religions are basically the same. Each speaks a similar message. All religions help their followers to live good lives, nudging persons toward superlative levels of evolutionary development.

Dr. Rantz graphically portrayed the great literature of all religions as being mutually harmonious by projecting

sections of great spiritual writings on the overhead pro-
jector, indicating their similarities. I had read the *Upani-
shads*, the *Ghita*, some Vedantic literature and sections of
the *Tibetan Book of the Dead* on my own. After one of
her classes I also added a *Koran* and a *Bible* to my
shelves, and promptly dismissed any lingering beliefs regarding the uniqueness of any great religious teacher,
including Christ, from my mind.

John was a Buddhist who ate only vegetables and wandered for long periods in the Nevada desert where he
frequently ate Peyote Buttons. I decided to add my
respect for theosophy to my respect for Theravadin Buddhism and concentrated on integrating the two into a
lifestyle of passive nonresistance and vegetarianism, but
I was never really very good at living either.

I dutifully read Carlos Castanada's *A Separate Reality*
and *The Journals of Don Juan* in response to a request
from my friend, but I never found them very interesting.
John and I spent long evenings together at an apartment
on Sierra Street watching the sun go down over beautiful
Mount Rose and other Sierra Nevada mountains, dreaming about the time when somehow there would be peace
on earth and dissolution of racial prejudice. Wouldn't it
be terrific if we somehow could help evolve into that ultimate harmony with his universe for which we both
yearned?

David Charlet ingested more hash, grass, mescaline,
and acid than anyone I had ever met. He seemed hooked
on drugs but not any particular kind. He went for what
was available. Moving into the apartment downstairs, he
often spaced out on some form or another of hallucinogenic
drug. He delighted in playing *Thus Spoke Zarathustra*
and *The Rites of Spring* on the stereo full blast, while

other friends spoke of him as somewhat strange. Huxley's *Doors of Perception* was one of his favorite books, and reading it instilled in me a deep curiosity about what it would be like to take a mescaline trip.

Virtually no experience attainable on the college campus eluded me. Oddly enough, the most significant one I had was some sort of "spiritual high" on cocaine. Grass could be easily purchased from Dave at $10.00 a lid. Dope smoking was no longer even a novelty. It was a normal part of many students lives. They, like me, considered lecture classes sessions of torture, lasting from one to three hours at a sitting. Thus we no longer simply grinned and bore it. We grinned and floated over them. "Orange Sunshine" was the best acid trip you could buy for the money. Sixty dollars purchased twenty "tabs" for a "four-way hit." Still, one six-hour acid experience seemed enough for me. I was leary of the hallucinogens anyway.

Homosexual encounters seldom occurred. They appeared in my mind to be chance experiences which left me always too soon in touch with a basic loneliness I was trying hard to forget. Even with sex, there seemed to be a morning after. Then, of course, there was the long haul until the next encounter. True, my resolution not to sleep with anyone I didn't love had been thrown out the window long ago, but what was sex without Mr. Right, and he certainly wasn't around.

One afternoon I was bored beyond belief. David dropped by the apartment and offered me some good acid if I would accompany him to a buddy's room at the dorm. Why not, I decided? Perhaps I'd find some sort of spiritual or validating experience on the stuff yet. I agreed and we headed off.

Over the door of one student room a large red mask of Satan's head with large black horns hung in stark contrast to the pale and dusty wall. This was it. We knocked, entered, and began negotiating with a young sophomore. I knew very little about LSD except for a few scary stories friends had told me, and that the "going rate" was the same all over campus. We settled on some unknown variety this time, paid the bucks, and "split."

Dave gave me my share—one tablet—and departed to be alone. He enjoyed his trips more that way when on strange varieties of hallucinogenics. I decided to "trip" right away, since the boredom of my life was really getting to me.

Each tablet was a four-way hit! No one had told me! It was the same as Orange Sunshine in the amounts. I'd be up for almost twenty-four hours and I didn't even know what kind of trip I'd have. Damn, I thought. This was going to be a real bummer.

And so it was. Whatever I had ingested was terribly hallucinogenic and was "cut" or "laced" with speed (amphetamines). I was in real trouble. First, spatial and perceptual changes hit me. My emotional reactions were incredible. I became paranoid and virtually overcome with fear. Then I began to hallucinate visual images and impressions I was thinking. Each thought became "real" and not all of them were good by a long shot.

About twenty minutes more into the drug and I began to wonder if I would ever come down! Twenty-four hours was a period I couldn't even think about, a period of interminable length. Thoughts of the aftermath of the Atlanta Pop Festival literally ripped me apart. Would I lose my entire reasoning ability forever, as young people there had. But I had no way out. I was "up" and would

stay "up" until the acid decided to let me go. Would I try
to fly and kill myself as Art Linkletter's daughter had
done? It all seemed to be up to the drugs. I had sur-
rendered my will to the stuff the moment I "popped" it.
I was no longer in control of myself. Panic began to
overwhelm me.

Fighting paranoia, I phoned Shelly McGwinn. She
answered the phone in her usual, gentle manner. "Look,
Shell," I said. "I'm 'up' and it's a real bummer. I'm not
gonna make it without help. You've got to get me to a
hospital before I flip out and lose it for good. Please get
here quick!"

Five minutes later this friend who had always been the
person to know in a crisis (she was a student nurse),
assisted me into the car with no lecture and rapidly drove
off toward Washoe Medical Center. Everything seemed
alive. Lights blurred in a never-ending pattern of chaos.
Sounds blared in my ears creating confusion that seemed
to deafen me. Finally, we were there. I hopped out of the
car and ran across the street to the emergency room, hoping that no cars were coming but not sure that they
weren't either.

A few minutes later I lay on the emergency room table
while visual hallucinations enveloped me. Screaming for
Thorazine, I overheard a nurse telling a colleague what a
stupid jerk I had been for taking drugs. The images on
my mind, which I was beginning to think might be real,
were too horrible to speak about. Shelly's sister Darcy arrived in the room to help calm me. A plan formed in my
reeling mind.

"Look, Darcy," I said in the general direction of the
consoling friend. "Will you kill me if I don't come
down?" I gazed straight into her now-beautiful-blue

eyes. "Kill me, Darcy, if I've blown it for good. Don't let me hang on the meat rack in some psycho ward somewhere forever. You've just got to kill me if I don't come down. You believe in mercy killing," I added, "don't you?"

A doctor checked my pulse. Panic seized me once again. "Put me in restraints, Doc," I cried. "Oh, God, I don't know what I'd do if I hurt anyone." Questions spun through my head. "Doc, hey, Doc, what keeps my heart going?" I inquired in a stupor, now that the Thorazine had begun to enter my system. (He had given me 100 milligrams, I believe.) Fear spurred me on to another thought. "Doc," I yelled, "Doc, what happens if my heart stops beating now?" On and on this nightmare continued. Second after second, minute after minute, hallucinations persisted, until finally time simply appeared to have no meaning. I honestly began to wonder again if I had taken the ultimate trip, the one from which I'd never return, blowing my mind permanently.

No, an hour later it was over. I had reacted well to the Thorazine. I was down. Fortunately, when the hospital personnel released me, no criminal charges were filed against me by the police. If I'd been arrested, I think I'd have committed suicide in the cell. It would have been more than I could bear at the time.

Once home in my apartment again, I promised (and meant it) that I would never try drugs again. Shelly made me swear on "all that was holy" and I was in just the frame of mind to agree. This was one promise I little realized then I would keep, not out of goodness, but out of fear. But my bout with the acid was not finished yet!

Awakening from my sleep in a cold sweat, I lost touch with reality. A series of flashbacks washed over me. It was just as if I were on the acid again, only this time I had taken nothing. My system was somehow reacting to the trauma that I had put it through. Again intense fear enveloped me. What if I hurt myself or someone else? Anxiety set in and never left me from that day forward. Forty-five minutes of what was to have been stolen pleasure turned into weeks of agonizing flashbacks so encompassing that I could not leave the house without heart palpitations, numbness over my entire body, and hyperventilation.

Finally, after months of this torture, I could stand it no longer. Life had been difficult enough for me when things were going "well." Now with this new and deeper burden to bear there was absolutely no point in living at all. My last reserves of fragile hope were completely eroded. Suicide beckoned, and I saw it as a happy alternative to my now worthless life.

What a birthday present, I thought to myself. Twenty-four years to the day after I had been born into this lousy world, I was giving myself the gift of death as a birthday celebration. I was alone, lost, an ready for the big trip. Hopefully it would end my suffering and not create more. Who knew? Maybe there really was an other side and things over there were better. Maybe, just maybe, Jesus was even God! Who knew? Certainly no one on this side did. A million things might have made my life different, I mused, yet here I was as I was. Something had to give.

Pausing a moment before slashing my wrists, rows of books lining the shelves caught my attention. "Go ahead," something inside me said. "Maybe, just maybe, there is something inside one of them that could help." I set the sharp blade on the table. Running my fingers through the largest stack of philosophy and theology books I have ever seen in one place outside of a library, my own resource shelves, I laughed cynically. Man's greatest philosophers, the world's greatest theologians, all vied for my attention. The issue at stake? My life. Who would save it for me? Who would give me the reason to live I so desperately needed. Who could do it? Who? "No one!" I cried. "Not one of you have it in you, do you? You're all worthless, all of you. You aren't worth the paper you write on," I yelled at one great thinker or another. Then I turned and walked toward the side of the living room where the sharp razor blade lay.

Muttering to myself again, I apologized to the books. It did seem sort of stupid, after all. Who could expect to find truth in a book all "pat" and laid out for you, just for the asking? What an absurd person I had become. What ridiculous demands I made on people, even worse than Howard Roark made on his clients.

Then, suddenly, a little book I had never read since I purchased it caught my attention. On its cover a bright rising sun dawning over a black mountaintop seemed to encapsulate my needs completely. Pulling it listlessly from the stack, its title offered exactly that for which my heart so longed. "*Good News for Modern Man,*" it read. It was the little New Testament I had purchased what seemed like years ago for the comparative religion class I was taking.

"Oh, come on, kid," a voice inside me shouted. "Jesus? You've heard the words of every so-called prophetic voice there is. Here's the game. A bunch of guys who supposedly have it all together morally tell you what your faults are. Then you "go down" in guilt because you're dumb enough to believe it. That's the way it went with the Catholic Church, your life in Buddhism, and even during your philosophical period with Rand."

Yet somewhere deep inside me another thought emerged. What if I "Cool-Hand Luked" it. In other words, what if I prayed asking God to reveal Himself to me some way right there in the room? If ever there was a time I was sincere about really giving in to God, this was it. I'd say it simply to Him in prayer just the way it was— no "Our Fathers", no "Hail Marys," and no "Glory Be's." If He responded, I would become His, forever.

"Lord," I prayed to Jesus, "prove to me that You're real and I'll give You my life. Amen." Deciding to read the Bible until "something happened," I curled up in a chair and opened to the Gospel of Matthew. "Great," I said to myself. "It's not in the King James English." I never would have read it if it were. Who could understand middle English with all its thees and thous, wilts, verilys, and cometh? Certainly not I.

Somewhere between Jesus' Sermon on the Mount and His commissioning the disciples to go throughout Israel preaching His message, He saved me! Although I did not know what that meant at the time, it actually, literally occurred. How, I didn't know!

Reading through Matthew's Gospel, Jesus simply emerged from the pages of the Bible, alive and real. He was no longer a myth or a legend. He was not one prophet among many. He was God in human form! Like Michelangelo's statue of David suddenly coming to life, the Spirit through faith resurrected Jesus in my heart from the written words which lay open before me. An intuitive knowledge of God flooded my consciousness convincing me beyond doubt that Jesus was real, alive, and in my room! All that He asked was for me to fulfill my

part of the bargain. With joy I did, becoming His for
eternity.

How could it have happened! Years of searching had
proven fruitless. A decade of church attendance yielded
nothing. And now, all of a sudden, I didn't just hope. I
knew with certainty as solid as the Palisades Cliffs that
Jesus was God. He must take my life, healing and cleansing and strengthing each warped and twisted thought,
every damaged and bruised emotion, all hopes and
dreams and aspirations. Whatever happened from this
moment on, only He could accomplish in me and
through me. Nothing else mattered, but Him alone.

Suddenly, catching me totally unaware, a "flashback"
occurred. For some unknown reason anger arose in my
heart. Loudly, with all the courage I could muster, I
ordered Satan to leave me alone, to return to hell from
whence he had come, and to cease his attack immediately! I yelled and screamed furiously at him, informing this now very real and dreaded enemy that he
could kill me, or cause me to end up in a mental hospital,
but that my spirit would never be his. The battle for my
soul was over and he had lost. Never again would anyone
else but Jesus be my God. He alone was my Savior for
eternity.

Unbelievably, just as rapidly as it had begun, the
"flashback" stopped! Never had I experienced anything
like it. Half an hour before I had not even believed Satan
existed, and now I was so convinced of his reality and
scheme to destroy me that I was shouting at him! Pro-
found physiological and emotional changes were precipitated by rebuking a spirit! "O my God," I couldn't help
praying, "how great and compassionate You are!"

What happened to the razor blade I cannot recall. Like

Paul's papers from the Roman government to the Pharisees in Damascus, it lay never discovered again. Along with it, every philosophy and theology book disappeared as well, only I knew of their fate. I burned each one in the apartment incinerator with childish delight. A catharsis as deep as my heart reflected itself in my home by the presence of a single Book on my shelves—the Bible alone.

5
You've Got to Be a Baby

Excommunication by Need

The first few years I spent with Christ at the Lake Street apartment I affectionately nicknamed "The Crib" was an agonizing period of spiritual surgery at the hands of the Great Physician. Contrary to the experience of many professing Christians I have met since that time, my initial steps with Jesus did not include great feelings or spiritual highs, nor did the Lord accomplish His work in my life primarily between 1:00 and 12:00 on Sunday mornings. He did not compartmentalize my life into a spiritual or religious Sunday segment and a secular or "normal" everyday one. Rather He began the process of integrating my emotional, mental, spiritual, physical, and social being into a somewhat more harmoniously functioning whole, centered always upon His indwelling personal presence. This was accomplished moment by moment, hour after hour, day by day.

I have to admit, however, that college studies did assume secondary priority for some time after my conversion. This was not because I became anti-intellectual. In fact, quite the contrary was true. For the first time ever I greatly appreciated learning. It was just that I needed a period of growth, a few years for God to lay a firm framework in my heart into which facts could be integrated in a truly Christian context.

God's Word became (and has remained) the real textbook of my life. Had circumstances been different, I might have entered a Bible school at once. Nothing was more thrilling to me than learning directly from the Lord Himself through His inspired Scripture. The same reality permeating the written account of Christ's life in the Gospel of Matthew since the night of my salvation extended to every verse of the Old Testament as well as the New.

I recognized immediately that each word in the Bible should be interpreted literally unless the context of the passage clearly indicated its allegorical nature. When absorbed with biblical studies, I was not involved in the idolatry of doctrine, nor in accepting unwarranted admonitions from a "paper pope." I was sitting at the feet of the Master, learning from God through the Word, all that He wished to teach me of Himself and His will.

During the first few days of my new life in Christ, I made a decision which was to remain a constant source of direction to me. Whatever contradicted biblical revelation, whether stated by pope or priest, professor or peer, would be immediately rejected. Jesus would not have allowed a false account of His life and mission to be written and believed by those who truly desired an unmitigated submission to Him as their God and Savior. I would tolerate no authority aside from that exercised by the Lord Himself channeled through a right understanding of Scripture.

Yet, even with the Bible as a constant companion, I had little knowledge regarding the nature of the spiritual experience I had undergone. My salvation had not been accomplished through the coming to life of any single text. It was the reality of Jesus acting in time, space, and history which struck me in Matthew's Gospel. Terms such as "born again," "saved," or "redeemed" were not as yet known to me. Catholics considered these experiences an adjunct either to birth or death and seldom employed biblical rhetoric in describing them. All I knew, however, was that Jesus is real and that my entire life now centered exclusively on Him. Added to this was my decision to accept the authority of biblical revelation over that which any person or supposed truth demanded of me. Little did I know that a test of this commitment would face me the next Sunday morning.

Praises of gratitude and prayers permeated with grace and thanksgiving poured from my heart as I walked the few short blocks separating my apartment from Our Lady of Wisdom Catholic Church about a week after my spiritual experience. Over and over my satisfied soul repeated the words of a favorite song, singing it to the Lord as a new and deeply treasured affirmation: "This world cannot be wrong, if in this world there is you."

Stepping into the simple but comfortable sanctuary, I could barely contain my bubbling emotions. This building was not large. Its brick walls were capped by lovely wooden beams. In the front, behind the altar, a large crucifix portrayed Jesus in agony on the cross. As the priest entered from the left in his striking green vestments, and the gold chalice glittered, flashing rays of sunlight and shadow pattern on the immaculate white altar cloth, I felt content. Now for the first time in my life, I had a right to be here. Indeed, I belonged here. This church and these fellow believers were the Lord's, and because they were His, they were mine as well. I was home at last, in the house of my God, surrounded by brethren who knew Him too—or was I? The introit began.

Exactly when the nagging doubts began to overwhelm me, I do not recall. Scriptures wouldn't leave me alone. I had read something about Jesus Himself being the great High Priest of the new covenant. Then there seemed to be the fact of His dying only once on Calvary. Where had I read those things? If only I could remember a little better the scattered bits of Scripture I had read. They seemed to clash horribly with the purported meaning of the ceremony at which I was now an uncomfortable participant.

Twenty minutes later, shortly before communion, I realized that I was a stranger in a familiar and yet now very foreign land. All the reality and spontaneity of my relationship with Jesus had become totally obscured through an attempted adherence to the unbiblical ritual of the mass. My spirit was crushed somehow. The other participants in this liturgy seemed to be dead puppets staging a cosmic melodrama. They were actors in a Sunday morning soap opera. Their words, and even their sitting, standing, and kneeling prayer postures, were prescribed for them since Vatican II in a neatly printed script called the *Mass Booklet*. Far from seeing true spirituality meaningfully expressed through this ritual, I discerned a sterile deadness, a mere adherence to an ecclesiastical tradition as abhorrent to the Lord as any heartless worship by the Jews had ever been.

Beneath what feeble attempts my mind could muster to justify this mechanical worship service, my heart said a definite "No!" to such a parody. I needed Bible teaching. I needed to share what God had done in my life last week so that anyone who might have shared something similar could help me understand what He had done. I needed prayer born out of the agony and triumph of the real life I now lived with Jesus. Finally, I admitted, I needed a friend, at least one other person who could perhaps identify and empathize with me as a new believer.

Kneeling in the rear of the church, that battle of Scripture and need continued. At last I could stand it no longer. Bolting from my pew, I couldn't tolerate this mass another moment. Half-walking, half-running from this cold Catholicism, once so much the core of my dreams and aspirations, I found myself a moment later in what I called the real world outside.

Dejected, overcome by depression, a new resolution grew within me as I sat on a tree stump flipping stones into the little pond on campus across from the church of my birth. Never again could I consider myself a Catholic! Tears poured forth from the depths of my soul. Although I could not then articulate the reasons nor verbalize the doctrine substantiating my feelings, something deep within me cried "Ichabod" at Catholicism. I knew with the same certainty that had enveloped me when I accepted Jesus as God that something was terribly wrong with the mass and whatever form of theology or "spirituality" had precipitated its celebration.

Jesus was free, open, and spontaneous. His Last Supper had occurred in the context of real life. His Sermon on the Mount took place outside. He seemed to teach from the depths of a heart attuned to God in the midst of an ever-present humanity appealing to His love from the pressing problems of a very real world. His encounters with men and women held a reality and spontaneity that formal prayer and ritual could never contain. Whatever sacraments there were, whatever kind of service He wished, must manifest a man's true spiritual life—love for God, dependence and need of His grace in a spontaneous manner overflowing with the thoughts, feelings, aspirations, tragedies, and victories real life always held.

Continuing to struggle with this problem, I reasoned that I was not the sole possessor of the Bible. There must be churches filled with those whose needs and insights based on Scripture paralleled my own. God had not commanded allegiance to any specific denomination, in the little study of the Bible I had done, as a prerequisite to eternal life. Instead, He seemed to long to be worshiped from the heart by all those who lived to love Him. No condemnation would arise from Him were I to leave the Roman Church. Sure, I would be excommunicated by the hierarchy of Catholicism here on earth, but what significance could such an anathema from those men mean to me now?

Jesus was real: He had come to me! I had already begun to realize something of the eternal importance of that fact during the brief time since my spiritual experience. I couldn't turn back. What good had all the masses, repetitious prayer, and penance ever done for me? The Lord had accomplished in my heart, in one moment of time, what years of monastic life had not even promised. Yes, I would leave the Roman Catholic Church. My quest for a truly scriptural assembly would begin with careful Bible study and find its fulfillment in some gathering of true believers only God alone now knew.

Like Paul in the Desert

"In my mind I launch a voyage, destiny unknown, discovery and exploration by the Spirit shown." Those words from the hit Christian musical, *The Apostle*, best describe my months of Bible study begun and continued daily after my departure from the Roman Catholic Church. Often six or eight hours would disappear before I realized I had not eaten. My sole goal in these sessions of communion with God was to accept honestly whatever leadings or callings resulted from coming to understand something of the Lord's character and will.

Christian radio implemented and greatly enhanced my personal journey into spiritual truth. "Conference Echoes" became my favorite program. On this show, some of the world's foremost Bible teachers offered sermons or lectures illustrating various biblical truths. I was seldom (if ever) aware of the backgrounds or denominational affiliations of these radio ministers. It simply did not make any difference to me. All their words I carefully measured against Scripture itself.

Without anyone in Reno with whom to fellowship, I turned to books. Francis A. Schaeffer's *The God Who Is There, He Is There and He Is Not Silent, Escape from Reason, Genesis in Space and Time,* and *The Mark of the Christian,* along with *True Spirituality,* served as real channels of liberation for me from the shackles of past secular philosophical thinking. They were used by the Holy Spirit to begin to separate the light from the darkness in my life.

Josh McDowell's *Evidence That Demands a Verdict*

struck a sharp blow at Satan's attempt to convince me
that Christianity has little historical foundation. Though
some presuppositionalists argue with what they term his
evidential approach to apologetics, all I knew was that I
understood his message. "The heart cannot rejoice in
what the mind rejects as false," he said. After each
chapter, my heart overflowed with a new and deeper joy
and insight into the historical Christ than I had ever
dreamed was possible.

Many of the professing Christians I met those years
seemed to consider "intellectual suicide" (my term for
their position) the real badge of superior holiness in the
Christian. I was forever being accused of being on a
"head trip" when I quoted Christian intellectuals. Yet, I
couldn't substantiate such an unscriptural attitude.

Were we not to love the Lord with all our minds, as
well as our hearts? How could I love Jesus and maintain
intellectual integrity without sitting at the feet of God,
the Holy Spirit, and benefiting from His teachings
ministered to me through the works of great saints whose
gifts of mind were much greater than my own? Wasn't
the brain (with all the knowledge it contained) of the
truly gifted Christian academician, as much hushed and
humbled before the Lord's throne as my less able one?
No, I ultimately decided, I would not quench Jesus' work
in my heart by an unbiblical repudiation of any truth
honestly finding its source in Him who called Himself
Truth and authored all truths scattered throughout His
universe.

Matthew Henry's and Jamison, Faucett, and Brown's
commentaries became as familiar to me as preprimer's
once were. They lay strewn about the floor of The Crib
with Vine's *Expository Dictionary* and *Strong's Concor-*

dance. Along with these tools of biblical study, I also found cassette tapes and a recorder a constant source of blessing. Various evangelical preachers offered an endless number of thirty-, sixty-, or ninety-minute sermons by mail. Seldom did a day go by that I did not listen to at least two or three of them exegete Scripture.

As always, I weighed every word of each sermon carefully against the Bible itself. I accepted nothing of what I was told by these men on tape without first fully understanding it and researching each verse meticulously. My final summation of most sermons was that they held much truth with which the Holy Spirit bore witness in my heart, plus many claims to truth which I could not accept. This was either because it was clearly contradicted by Scripture, or because I was not yet able fully to understand it. God led me into three approaches to biblically based claims for truth: (1) accept it, (2) reject it, or (3) wait until you understand it more fully. His guidance always took the form of line upon line, precept upon precept. Often one point would have to wait until He gave me another teaching on something else, then the first point would fit like a jigsaw puzzle into the incredible revelation of His character and will.

No Longer Gay

Not long after my salvation, I was reading through Paul's first epistle to the church at Corinth. As I concentrated intensely on each word, two verses stood out as if they were written in gold on the black background of my mind. Past experiences of this nature led me to believe that once again the Holy Spirit had an important lesson to teach me. Thus, I reread and exegeted 1 Corinthians 6:9-11 in depth:

Or do you not know that the unrighteous shall not inherit the kingdom of God? Do not be deceived; neither fornicators, nor idolators, nor adulterers, nor the effeminate [*malechoi*], NOR HOMOSEXUALS [*arsenkoitai*] nor thieves, nor covetous, nor drunkards, nor revilers, nor swindlers, shall inherit the kingdom of God. And SUCH WERE SOME OF YOU; but you were washed, but you were sanctified, but you were justified in the name of the Lord Jesus Christ, and in the Spirit of our God. (Emphasis added.)

The frist important point in these verses seemed to me to be the distinction that Paul was making between the homosexual who would not inherit the kingdom of God and the homosexual who had found Christ and was apparently no longer homosexual. The apostle's use of the aorist tense in the verse was most striking: "Such WERE some of you" (completed action in the past), he exclaimed triumphantly. But that is over with, finished, completed, indeed dead, for you have been washed, justified, and sanctified through your new experience of repentance from dead works and faith in the living God.

A study of the *Petristic Greek-English Lexicon* brought further light on the subject. The word for homosexual used here, although translated in several ways in our English versions of the Bible, referred to one who fulfilled the spirit of the prohibition of Leviticus 18:22:

You shall not lie with a male as one lies with a female; it is an abomination . . . .

and Leviticus 20:13:

If there is a man who lies with a male as those who lie with a woman, both of them have committed a detestable act . . . .

Obviously, Paul was asserting in the new covenant, the continuance of the moral law of the old covenant, thus his admonition to Timothy in 1 Timothy 1:8 (NIV):

> We know that the law is good if a man uses it properly. We also know that law is made not for good men but for lawbreakers and rebels, the ungodly and sinful, the unholy and irreligious; for those who kill their fathers or mothers, for murderes, for adulterers and...[homosexuals] for slave traders and liars and perjurers—and for *whatever else is contrary to the sound doctrine that conforms to the glorious gospel of the blessed God, which he entrusted to me* (emphasis added.)

I could not deny it. Homosexuality was declared in the Bible, both in the Old and New Testaments, to be sinful. It was contrary to the sound teaching which conforms us to the gospel, which Jesus gave, and Paul taught. Those who continued on in it would never inherit God's kingdom. Yet Paul knew some in Corinth who had made a decisive break with such sin and therefore were actually regarded as ex-homosexuals by him. Although at one time he was forced to say of these former gays,

> Therefore God gave them over in the sinful desires of their hearts to sexual impurity for the degrading of their bodies with one another. They exchanged the truth of God for a lie, and worshiped and served created things rather than the Creator—who is forever praised. Because of this God gave them over to degrading passions. Even their women exchanged the natural functions for those which are unnatural.... In the same way the men also abandoned natural relations with women and were inflamed with lust for one another. Men committed indecent acts with other men, and received in themselves the due penalty for their perversion (Romans 1:24-28, NIV).

he could now shout of them victoriously:

> Therefore, if any man is in Christ, he is a new creature;
> the old things passed away; behold, the new things have
> come.... These things are from God, who reconciled us to
> Himself through Christ (2 Corinthians 5:17, 18).

Truly, I was no longer a homosexual in God's eyes.
Surely, I had been washed, justified, and sanctified. Beyond dispute, as far as I was concerned, was the fact that
I had a new identity as a man in the Lord. All this was
certain in spite of what temptations from my lower carnal
nature might still remain to plague me and cause me to
cry out for grace from Jesus to live conditionally in light
of my new position in Him.

Not long after this exciting revelation, I was given
some literature written by proponents of what has come
to be known as the pro-gay movement. These tracts and
books grieved my spirit intensely with what I regarded as
their mixture of abstract subjective reasoning and humanistic psychological approaches. The authors of these
publications appeared to be employing such techniques
to substantiate the validity of continued involvement in
homosexual practices within what they termed "mo-
nogomous covenantal unions," even for those professing
a saving knowledge of Jesus Christ as their personal Lord
and Savior.

How could I read Malcom Boyd's incredible words
and remain unconcerned for him? He dared to state that
homosexuality can give rise to

> the fullest expression of universal solidarity with life—
> when one feels grateful to God for all of creation including
> one's own.

Continuing on in print he blesses homosexual unions and declares sex in such relationships to be "sacraments of the universal life force created by God."

Troy Perry's *The Lord Is My Shepherd and He Knows I'm Gay* filled me with such a pity for the founder of the Universal Fellowship of Metropolitan Community Churches that I felt constrained both by love for him and for Jesus to call this man and share by understanding of God's Word with him. Yet it soon became apparent to me in this dialogue that it would take a miracle of Jesus for us to come to agreement on this matter and that for reasons unknown to me such might not occur for a long, long time, if at all.

I continued trying to dialogue with pro-gay leaders by phone. I shall never forget the night I stood racked with sobs of grief as I shared my testimony with one the authors of *Is the Homosexual My Neighbor?* Nothing I said could convince her that she could not truly affirm homosexuals by affirming in them that which would ultimately destroy them—either here on earth or before the judgment seat of God. Always I seemed boxed into a frame of thinking by these authors who I did not espouse. It went something like this: "To be against homosexuality is to be against the homosexual." The once-gay-always-gay myth predominated. I could not break through.

Over and over again I attempted to contact Ralph Blair, a professingly Christian psychotherapist who had written a booklet entitled *An Evangelical Look at Homosexuality*. These efforts proved fruitless. He continued to spend much of his time counseling gays that involvement in homosexual acts was in accordance with the will of God for them.

Often my discussions with pro-gay, yet proportedly Christian, theologians became enmeshed in a subtle web of historical/cultural, rhetorical/grammatical, personal/experiential justification for their views. They appeared almost blatantly and openly unwillingly to consider the research I had compiled on the linguistic and historical aspects of the subject under the direction of such wonderful Greek scholars as Mr. Goodrich of Mulntnoma School of the Bible in Portland, Oregon, and others.

How grateful to God I became after these experiences with pro-gay advocates to discover the work of men like Don Williams (*The Bond That Breaks*), John White (*Eros Defiled*), Kent Philpott (*The Third Sex, The Gay Theology*), Tim La Haye (*The Unhappy Gays*), Mike Bussee and Jim Kasper (*Melodyland's Exit Team*), Frank Worthen (*Love in Action Newsletter*), and the Fitzwaters (*Jesus Outreach Center*). With tears and prayer, through suffering and persevering effort, by personal testimony or counseling experience, these men—many of whom had been publicly attacted and maligned for their upholding the testimony of Scripture—continued to wash the feet of the ex-gay Christian like myself, as they poured forth a virtual stream of living water to the gay still bound in the bondage of iniquity and the gall of bitterness by the homosexual compulsions I had so recently seen shattered in my own life and the lives of so many others.

With my heart firmly fixed upon the enduring and unchanging truths of God's Word, and my eyes often filled with tears as I observed the scars on my arms and legs which served as grim reminders to me of the awful price paid for my past homosexual sin, I could do no less than commit myself fully to making myself available to any other gay or ex-gay Christian in need of ministry, as these other godly men had done.

Healing of the Emotions: A Gradual Process

Like Paul, I thought Jesus was preparing me for work and service in His kingdom. Yet, His preparation was not to be limited to biblical revelation. Emotional development appeared equally important to Him. Anxiety characterized my emotional state. The acid I had ingested was said to have been "cut" or "laced" with speed (amphetamines). "Rushes" or anxiety attacks did not subside at first, even though no flashbacks ever occurred after my initial deliverance the night of my salvation. Still I was a nervous person and would remain so for many years.

My immediate emotional needs centered on finding a way to handle the nervousness which had remained so uncomfortably within me. Deciding I must depend solely on the Holy Spirit for support, I simply prayed each time tenseness arose. Placing myself in the Lord's capable hands allowed me to trust His willingness and ability to control my damaged emotions and produced tangible, almost miraculous results. I could actually feel God at work within me. From periods of near panic, in only a few seconds of prayer, I would be led into a state of almost perfect emotional peace. I stood squarely on the Scriptures at such times, casting all my care upon Him, knowing that He cared for me. By His grace I determined to be anxious about nothing but in all things make my request for peace known to Him with praise and thanksgiving.

I had no doubt in my mind that the Lord could and would assist me during such anxiety attacks. Yet a feeling crept over me that I might somehow be tempting God. I came to wonder about this, especially when the nervousness always returned to haunt me once again. Perhaps the Lord would grant a more complete healing, a once-and-for-all victory over this anxiety through a psychiatrist. Like Paul I besought Jesus to take my nervousness away and nothing happened. Perhaps God would deliver me further through professional help.

And so it was I found myself one day in the office of Dr. Montgomery, a respected psychiatrist in Reno. Dr. Montgomery listened with interest as I related the facts concerning my past life in a somewhat reluctant manner. I became increasingly cautious during the therapy session because of his strange eye movements. Each time I mentioned the Lord he turned his eyes away from me staring down into the parking lot six floors below. A graduate of Stanford Medical School and one of the best psychiatrists in Reno, he was nevertheless unsaved.

Soon I began to feel as if he interpreted my steady stream of references to Jesus and His presence in my life in a caustic or cynical manner. Was he assessing this as an indication of severe psychological illness? Admitting my homosexuality and contemplation of suicide prior to conversion made me especially uncomfortable, even though I affirmed that no physical involvements had occurred since my conversion.

Finally I couldn't tolerate sitting in his office any longer. Hadn't he said that he was unable to promise any cure for my gayness? I certainly wasn't being liberated from anxiety under his rather bizarre gaze out the large windows of his luxurious office at each mention of Jesus. Accepting a prescription for two large bottles of Stelazine I assured the doctor that the proper amount of $50 for the one hour session would be paid as promised and left the suite of expensively furnished rooms which comprised his office.

"Physician Slays Wife and Kills Self: Two Children Survive Reign of Terror!" Those words screamed at me from the front pages of our local newspaper only a few mornings after my visit to the psychiatrist. On the right-hand column of the page, Dr. Montgomery's picture unmistakably identified him as the person referred to so tragically in the rest of the article. A deep compassion for this unsaved man overwhelmed me. Focusing hostility he could not handle upon himself and his wife, my doctor had ended both their lives. I couldn't help wondering if his staring off into the parking lot at each mention of suicide during our interview was precipiated by some carefully hidden contemplation of the course of action mentioned in the article which he had been harboring during our session together.

Jesus' leading through this seemed clear, I should continue to pray when anxiety attacks arose, trusting in him alone for my cure. Perhaps He would send a Christian therapist my way in time. The Lord's grace was sufficient in my weakness. If this "thorn in the flesh" was something to be borne for a while or for the rest of my life on earth, I would have His grace in dealing with it. I flushed the contents of both bottles of Stelazine down the toilet.

Still Standing in the Corridor

C. S. Lewis said it best in one of his books. "A man can stand in the corridor of the church for awhile, but sooner or later he must enter through one of its denominational doors." I had been deeply committed to finding a church home ever since I had left Catholicism, yet for an ex-Catholic the world of contemporary Christianity seemed awesome and even frightening at times.

Pentecostal prayer meetings were my greatest love at first. I've never imagined angels singing with greater beauty than that of my Pentecostal brethren when they offered their praises to God in the little house chapel I was attending each Monday. Always my spirit was elevated by this gathering. All the spontaneity of worship which the Roman Catholicism I had known suppressed by liturgical ritual was given an adequate expression here. Biblical rhetoric and holy embraces were two signs that an attempted return to primitive Christianity was something most Pentecostals deeply yearned for. Yet gradually an awareness crept over me that this was not where I belonged in the family of God.

Perhaps the greatest myth of the movement to which I could not adhere was the belief that every believer must have a "second work of grace," termed the "baptism of the Holy Spirit," and that this experience was (must be?) accompanied by the evidence of speaking in tongues. Because I could neither justify this assumption biblically nor conjure it up experientially, my involvement with Pentecostalism gradually terminated. At first I had been treated with condescension. Later I was exhorted as a chronic seeker. Finally I was discarded as a spiritual second-class citizen, obviously on some form of intellectual "head trip."

Actually, although I was not to remain within the confining structural myths of neo-pentecostalism, I was charismatic, and always remained so. While I could not justify a second work of grace as normative and necessary in the Christian life, nor could I believe that tongues was

God's will for each believer, I learned much from members of the movement which contributed immensely to my understanding of the gifts and callings within the kingdom of God. I did accept the validity of many experiences that the Pentecostals claimed originated from the Holy Spirit. But their theology seldom matched these experiences. It added a burden on young Christians such as myself, which I found precipitated much insecurity and instability in the heart. My last involvement in a Pentecostal prayer meeting was a particularly disasterous encounter.

Nancy had claimed the gift of prophecy for many years. Her two sons also claimed this gift as well. The Cames opened their home to all believers, regardless of denominational affiliation, every Monday evening. "Closet" and open Pentecostals from various churches in Reno gathered there to worship in the generally accepted manner of the Pentecostals.

As we lifted our arms to the Lord while sitting in a small circle one evening, Nancy began to give evidence of some supernatural spiritual manifestation. Gazing up toward the ceiling, she said, "I feel something on my head? What is it?" I sensed that this question might have been precipitated by a prior prohecy given by her son Chad, earlier that evening, stating that the whole gathering would be "clad in the full armor of God" that night. Not knowing how to respond to this intelligent and creative woman, now somehow lost in reverie. I simply sat and stared at her in wonder.

Then, one by one, each person at the meeting offered an explanation to her question. The first began, "Why ... why it's the helmet of salvation!" From another place in the circle a brother now responded, "I feel something on my chest? What is it?" A sister replied, "It's the breastplate of righteousness." On and on this process continued until every Christian in the group claimed to be "clad in the full armor," thus fulfilling the prophecy given an hour before. Every Christian there, that is, except me! I felt nothing anywhere. Once again I was the third wheel, the ugly duckling, the wet blanket.

Rising from my place on the floor, I decided to pray for a while downstairs in the living room. Back and forth across the carpet I walked begging the Lord to assist me in understanding just what had transpired in the chapel above. Finally, I concluded (whether rightly or wrongly) that I simply couldn't know, but that whatever it was that I had just witnessed had not had God as its source.

Heading back upstairs to the chapel, I requested a hearing by the entire gathering. Nancy (the group's unofficial leader) nodded hesitantly, and I read from the epistle to the Colossians, exhorting each believer in the room not to take his stand on visions he had seen, being puffed up and inflated in his carnal mind without cause. The reaction was explosive. Before I could finish offering the needed exhortation, Nancy said, "I knew I shouldn't have let you teach. I just knew it." Chad escorted me physically from the room and drove me home with a stiff command never to return again.

Although doctrinal differences and inexplicable experiences I often did not share accounted for some of my dissatisfaction with neo-Pentecostalism, other ideas came to me which are just as forcefully severed whatever ties I might have attempted to keep with the movement. I sensed a subtle form of ascetic mysticism pervading many assemblies. It did not seem to reflect adequately a proper balance in the vertical and horizontal relationships inherent in the Christian life—those between the believer and God and the believer and his brother. This imbalance manifested itself in a superficiality of relationship with fellow Christians, not in accordance with the biblical injunctions to show our love to one another not only in word but in deed and truth.

Many times I was greeted with a hearty, "Praise the Lord, Jesus loves you," upon entering the prayer meeting on Monday night, yet, during the week no one ever visited my home. Nor was any real attempt made to share Scripture or prayer with me over the phone. I was loved by God, or so I was told, but was I loved by Nancy and Chad? I really didn't think so. If so, I had no way of telling that I was. Wasn't love something more than a greeting casually exchanged upon entering a prayer meeting?

Attendance at formal institutionalized services of the Pentecostal movement reinforced my belief that God was not leading me into its ranks either. At such gatherings (which I sought out after reading David Wilkerson's *The Cross and the Switchblade*), teachers monopolized the meetings with their gift, proving in sermon after sermon that the entire Bible was meant for today. What God had done in Acts as well as in the other early churches He could do here. Yet Paul's injunctions on church order in 1 Corinthians 12 to 14 were neglected or openly rejected as not applicable to the situation at hand. These zealous believers appeared to desire the Spirit's "fullness" in their midst, but they certainly did not seem to want the Spirit's discipline in their hearts.

Many times women and men spoke in tongues together all at once. Seldom did I ever hear an interpretation. This was unnecessary, I was exhorted. Interpretations were for the gift of tongues. What I was hearing was the private prayer language all could have if they only sought it, they told me. I couldn't help wondering why a private prayer language would be used publicly without interpretation, but felt it would be better not to press the point.

I created additional problems for them when I attempted to share my view that women maintained an equality of acceptance but a distinction of role in the church, just as they did in marriage, and that because Paul pointed toward the natural law and the presence of angels, not to cultural norms as evidence that they should be veiled in public worship, much of their key leadership and functioning was undisciplined. Now I was a male chauvinist and legalist!

One problem with the Pentecostals I observed was their superficial Bible study and lack of personal application of the teachings in the Word. Added to this was the pervasive feeling that they had "arrived." They had achieved a superior holiness and place in the kingdom of God by their second blessing experience. Since I had not experienced the second work of grace nor the commencement of tongues in my life, most of what I said they discarded out of hand. Perhaps it was this "Pentecostal Pride," as I called it, which made me feel alienated from the other believers more than any other single factor.

My last encounter with the movement in its "churched" form came when another Christian brother and I decided to share in the service of a Pentecostal church not far from my apartment. It was at this meeting that the final embers of my now dimly burning hope to find a place in Pentecostalism were completely extinguished. I was deeply grieved.

During the meeting, an evangelist-teacher glared out

at his congregation and said, "There is a woman here
from India. If we would have prayed the way God wants
us to pray, He would have given us the gift of tongues.
Then we would have been able to communicate with her.
You believe this, don't you?"

For what seemed like an eternity, that long bony evangelist's finger swept the congregation. Please, Lord, I
prayed, don't let it stop at me! But there it was, pointing
squarely at my place. Following it up the long arm,
chest, and chin of the austere brother, I finally met his
eyes. His question could not be taken as rhetorical. He
was waiting with upraised eyebrows and a grim scowl,
somewhat impatient at the delay. He had expected a
ready and positive response from me. I gulped! How did
we know that the woman didn't speak English? Maybe
she was already saved, Spirit-filled, and an ardent
tongues speaker herself! What if it was not God's will for
her to receive the gospel message in just that manner? I
just couldn't honestly give a pat "yes" answer to the
question.

"Well, sir," I croaked. "Well ... no, not necessarily,
sir," I finished weakly. Not taking another moment's
pause, the evangelist shouted at me with all the fury he
could muster (which seemed considerable to one such as
I, so short a time out of high church Catholicism).
"Young man, meet me after the service in the back room.
I want to talk to you! You're filled with evil spirits."
Turning abruptly to the audience, he continued with his
message. Two deacons dressed in black loomed omi-
nously close by. I felt myself among the damned!

After dismissal, the evangelist marched down the aisle
toward my seat. "Get up there into that room," he commanded loudly enough for any who had missed his prior

exhortation, an hour earlier, to hear. "I want to talk to you."

I walked slowly toward the counseling room and entered, paying close attention to the number of doors and windows available for a hasty exit if the need arose.

"Kneel down!" the evangelist shouted, as I sweated profusely, terrified beyond words, at his harsh rebukes. But kneel I did, too frightened to run.

Just as my knees hit the floor, the "unpardonable sin" became evident. My three button-jacket parted and a half-empty package of Salem cigarettes began what seemed to me a slow motion journey to the floor. As a baby Christian, the world's knowing I smoked didn't bother me, but it wasn't the world that mattered just then. The world I could handle, but the evangelist's face turning purple and then almost black at the sight of those cigarettes, now on the floor at last, compounded with my prior offense petrified me. I couldn't have moved a muscle if I had tried. I was literally frozen in a kneeling position.

"God can never have anything to do with you as long as you smoke," shouted the evangelist furiously. "You are filled with demons and are in dire need of the baptism of the Holy Spirit for deliverance from such sinful habits!" He continued screaming and yelling at me for perhaps ten minutes, treating me as if I were a postulant in a religious community, a trainee in boot camp, or a homosexual who had just propositioned his son, with a tone that I thought was reserved for the concluding minutes of a hellfire sermon.

Finally, unable to tolerate my emotions and this brother's hateful attitude another moment, I rose, stared him square in the face, and stated loudly, "God might not have anything to do with me because I have nicotine stains on my hands, but he had a lot to do with Paul and he had bloodstains on his. And you know," I concluded, "He never achieved His purposes in that murderer's life by being obnoxious toward him, as you are being toward me!"

Horrified at my own audacity, I ran off into the now darkened city to look for my friend who had left some time ago. Sauntering slowly along the deserted sidewalks, I began to assess my place in the institutionalized church of the Pentecostal movement. I realized it was over. I would never return. No, I didn't believe that all Pentecostal assemblies were exactly like this one, yet I knew that some of them shared its propensity toward psychologically destructive interpersonal encounters. I couldn't risk another such experience in the future.!

At that public service, I had received a psychological wound that would take some time to heal. It appeared as a feeling of estrangement, a loss of self-worth and self-respect that frightened me. This assembly was not mine. It belonged to the elders and members, content with doctrines it cherished and practiced. Their overemphasis on demonic activity, unscriptural monopolization of the meeting by a single gift, (evangelism, healing, or preaching, usually) along with the harsh looks of condemnation received from fellow worshipers after my response to the evangelist, convinced me beyond a doubt that this was not where I belonged.

Discipline seemed a point of special consideration, I thought. The "holiness" orientation, bordering on legalism which I experienced in that assembly conjured up all sorts of fears within me. It turned Christianity into nothing more than what Catholicism had always been, a cause for self-condemnation, insecurity, and slavish obedience to cultural norms transformed into biblical absolutes.

In my heart I knew there must be some balance between "cheap grace" and "heart holiness." If believers were not challenged to the sanctity without which no man shall see God, they would remain always displeasing to Him. Yet if they were provoked to anger by a discipline devoid of love, and not administered in proportion to their offenses, they would lose faith in God's tender love for them. Scriptural discipline seemed best applied in the manner described in the Bible. Any deviation from its form and spirit as expressed there seemed devastatingly counterproductive.

Perhaps, I concluded, a non-Pentecostal assembly would be more in tune with God's will and Word. Maybe, just maybe, that was where I belonged. This evening encounter made me determined to find out if such was indeed the case.

Perhaps This Door?

Not long after my final, traumatic departure from the neo-Pentecostal church I had been attending, I was invited by a sister to visit her congregation's Sunday morning worship service. Because the assembly she attended wasn't far from my apartment, and because I had resolved to find a place somewhere within Christianity's institutionalized church structure in which I could experience some sense of belonging, I decided to accompany her.

This church's sanctuary looked very much like the Catholic one's I was used to. Huge wooden beams arched toward a central point in an open ceiling, which was both ornate and beautiful. Behind the wooden platform, upon which the emblems for communion had been placed, a round stained-glass window pictured Jesus kneeling in prayer by a rock in Gethsamane. Row after row of hard wooden pews lined the main worship area. Two groups of brethren, clad in formal blue silk choir robes with gold trim, sat silently behind the pastor, a rotund middle-aged minister who was now standing in his pulpit ready to begin the service.

First the congregation was invited to join in several songs. Then the elder's sermon commenced. It focused on what I later learned was a standard plea for anyone in the congregation who did not know Christ to come forward and express faith in Him, for He was indeed the Savior of the world. This lasted for almost an hour. An offering plate was passed, and I thought we were ready for dismissal—but I was mistaken.

All the lights, except for one which illumined the picture of Christ in stained glass at the front of the church, were extinguished. Little cups of grape juice and white bread were distributed to each person in the sanctuary. The pastor disappeared from the pulpit, and I couldn't figure out for the life of me where he had gone! Then I heard his voice coming from somewhere behind me, singing softly and beautifully. He was praising God in song from the rear choir loft as each member of His flock worshiped the Lord silently, while consuming the symbols of the Lord's Supper. I was deeply moved by this reverent communion service reminiscent in so many ways of the Catholic masses of my childhood.

Still, as I look back now, I was not content with such a worship service. Here, even in evangelical Protestantism, I was faced with a more or less ritualized form of ministry to the Lord. No opportunity was given for individual prayers from the congregation, and the large number of people present would have militated against honest sharing on a deep personal level. Only the minister's gift functioned, and even at that, why did he assume an evangelist's role, preaching what I called a "simple salvation sermon"? Was Brother Ralph really using a charismatic gift of evangelism, or did he have pastoral and teaching gifts? First Corinthians 14:26 kept nagging at me. "When you assemble, *each one* has a pslam, has a teaching, has a revelation, has a tongue, has an interpretation. Let all things be done for edification". The spontaneity of the nonchurched Pentecostal movement, was gone. I missed it desperately. There must be some way, I thought, to avoid Pentecostal extremes and yet realize the biblical forms of the movement, making the service truly a charismatic expression of the Holy Spirit.

After the service, everyone was invited to the church basement for fellowship. Now, I thought, I could really begin to make friends with other Christians. Here I could feel at home, initiating new and challenging relationships with fellow believers. Sure, I was nervous, but never one to feel too uncomfortable when engaged in sharing, I knew that I could make out okay, or could I?

The basement of the church was a mass of chattering people precariously balancing doughnuts and coffee on laps and chairs. Everyone seemed fully occupied, conversing with family, friends, and relatives. I stood huddled in a corner, so filled with anxiety that I almost spilled the coffee from my cup each time I attempted to bring it to my lips. For over fifteen minutes I waited for someone to approach me. No one did! Then, finally, not to be mastered by the situation that easily, I began to mill about, standing close first to this group and then to that one. Yet each time I did so, I found myself looking into a gentleman's shoulder blades or a woman's French bun. Ten more long minutes (and four years of prior communications training) assured me that I was a new, but not very welcome, face and nothing more. I found my friend Nancy and asked her if it would be all right to leave.

Discussing my experience with Nan over a cup of tea back at the apartment, I was surprised to hear her affirm my perceptions. "Yes," she nodded agreebly, "I've had the same questions about the worship service myself." "But," she added almost a challenge, "it's not the morning assembly which keeps me at New Hope. It's *His House*."

Ready for anything, now that my earlier views concerning the Sunday morning meeting had been confirmed, I offered, "Go ahead. Hit me. I'm game."

"Well, you see, Kev," Nan stated slowly, "a lot of the older people enjoy the service to which I took you. But young members like to gather at a house close by the church on Sunday evenings for a less formal time of fellowship, teaching, and prayer." Realizing that my plans for the evening had already been set for me, I awaited the inevitable question I knew wouldn't be long in coming. Thus I found myself grinning as Nan said, "Want to go with me tonight, Kev, do you, huh?"

Her eyes beckoned with a plea that a real Christian could hardly refuse.

"Of course," I replied. "How much time do I have to get ready?"

Nan rose from her chair, as if to rush away lest I change my mind. "We'll meet at 5:30. Everything begins at 6:00. See you then."

As she turned and headed out the door with a quick wave, I said to the Lord, "Okay, Jesus, I promised to do whatever it takes to find a church home, so here I go again. You're not going to let me down, are You?"

His House that night was the greatest single encounter I had experienced with a group of people since I had accepted Christ as Savior. A two-story home had been converted into a meeting place for about seventy teenagers who sang praises to the Lord with a warmth and spontaneity I found incredibly enjoyable. Two brothers, who were about my own age, taught lessons on the Book of Revelation. Each gave of his wisdom freely and happily. Finally, not long before the meeting came to a reluctant close, in what seemed to me to be only a few minutes, individual prayer poured forth from hearts which appeared to have been genuinely touched by God. I had found my place in the kingom of God. Embraces were exchanged as the young believers expressed a love for one another that had not been created in the meeting alone. They knew one another and had ties which task-oriented groups could not adequately express but which freed them to be involved in such encounters meaningfully. These kids, still almost children, actually possessed a fellowship as biblical as any I had ever dared hope to find!

Nan didn't really have to ask, but I knew she would, and sure enough she did. "Hooked?" she inquired, noticing the broad grin and relaxed posture I had assumed while slurping the last strawberry from the bottom of the soda glass at the *Denny's* restaurant, where we sat surrounded by many of the *His House* bunch.

"Sure am," I replied. "It pays to leave yourself vulnerable, reaching out to risk sometimes, doesn't it?"

She nodded happily and squeezed my hand gently. "You see, Kev, maybe there is a place, even for you, in the church after all."

I agreed completely, but grew oblivious even to the chattering of the teenagers surrounding me on every side, lost in an attempt to understand the components of the *His House* meeting that had so intrigued me.

Why was individual prayer and an informal atmosphere, along with honest dialogue between believers, characteristic of young people in both the Pentecostal and non-Pentecostal churches? I wondered. Only the prayer meeting of the neo-Pentecostal movement incorporated this genuineness. Why didn't more church meetings take place in house settings? Why had I found myself relegated to the youth group by the Lord in my search for a place in the assembly. Was it because I myself was immature, or was it becaues there was something even Jesus had noticed in the young which I found compelling, a tell-it-like-it-is reality without which I couldn't feel comfortable in any group. These questions came on and on in a steady stream, but a spilled Coke, and a paper airplane constructed from a place mat landing on my shoulder, convinced me it was time to leave further meditation on these points to a more appropriate time and setting. Our kids were asking for rides home, and I knew we mustn't make them late.

My involvement with *His House* soon became one of the greatest joys of my week. Teaching was not a new endeavor for me, but it was definitely a happy one. Loneliness almost disappeared from my life, as I became immersed in relating to the kids. If I wasn't participating in the formal assembly of the church on Sunday mornings, at least I was using my spiritual gift in the evening.

Our friendships were not limited to this period between 6:00 and 7:00 p.m., however. The young people called me up periodically through the week to share this problem or that with a person they knew loved them deeply in the Lord.

Much to my delight and surprise, I had become a popular member of the *His House* gang! Incredibly (to me) a once rejected and lonely young man became an integral part of a large group of people. The teenagers loved the way I taught, joking and sharing informally with them during the studies, answering their questions, affirming them, and just making learning a joyful experience. The Lord, from whom my teachings always came, blessed them, and I began to feel as if I really belonged with this congregation.

Only one thing disturbed my otherwise tranquil relationship with the kids. As I became acquainted with them beneath the veneer of the smiles, prayers, and even Christian rhetoric they constantly maintained, I learned that most were new converts. A majority of them had unsaved parents to whom they had difficulty relating. Some had been, and even occasionally now were, involved in drugs. Sex was an ever-present option and problem. I recognized their desperate need to integrate basic Christian values and principles in their hearts. Bible teaching must become more relevant. It must include discussion of how scriptural truth could be applied in the warp and woof of these youngsters lives if they were to avoid the pitfalls of adolescence, if they were to live their daily lives in a manner glorifying to God. Their desire might be centered on learning about prophecy and becoming excited about the imminent return of Christ (in which I too also believed deeply). But their obvious struggle with temptation and sin indicated that a study of Romans 7 and 8 and similar passages should have a higher priority. Not only must we believe in the Lord's second coming, we must be prepared for it by lives lived in holiness and righteousness before Him, day and night, until He arrives.

Deciding to approach the two older teachers with my insights I arranged to meet with them, and the pastor as well, one evening at the parsonage.

Brother Ralph listened with the same mild interest he usually displayed over such matters as I related my perceptions of the *His House* group. Relying heavily on personal conversations I had had with several of the young brothers and sisters, yet without revealing names, I shared my understanding of their need for teaching on the basics of Christian living. It was crucial, I confided, to convey to these kids the necessity and manner of relying totally on God's power, of putting to death the deeds of the flesh by the power of the Holy Spirit. They must be taught principles of prayer and Bible study, so that they could grow spiritually and truly live for Christ at home and at school. Concluding my little sermonette with a statement of my deep love and affection for the teens, I turned to Mike and Don, expecting some reinforcement concerning what I had just said. None was forthcoming.

The pastor had initiated *His House* himself. He stated that it was successful and growing. He had left the decision of what was to be studied in the Bible up to the young people themselves. They had chosen the Book of Revelation; he had not. Until a thorough study of this prophetic work had been completed at *His House*, and the students themselves requested it, no change in the curriculum would be forthcoming. Of course, he added, if either of the other two brothers had anything to share it would be taken into consideration.

Mike and Don nodded toward the pastor affirmingly. They agreed completely with his views. There was no need to change the lessons. My perceptions were an over-reaction, perhaps, to intense involvement with one or two of the kids, plus my own theology. If I didn't like things the way they were—well. . . .

My heart sank. Only three times before in my Christian life had I had to face such a decision, first in leaving the church of my birth, then in leaving the Pentecostal prayer meeting, then my departure from churched Pentecostalism, and now this new situation. If I was to give the young people what they needed, I would be asked to leave. If I didn't, I would be responsible to the Lord for not having met their needs and for resisting His leading. Submission to the pastor and to my fellow teachers would mean disloyalty to Christ in my eyes. I knew that the teens must learn how to live with sanctity in God's sight. I couldn't turn my back on that fact. Within a few months, I felt sure, some of them would be shipwrecked in their faith.

My decision was careful and deliberate. I attempted to convey it in love. I would give the pastor and the other teachers one month to evaluate their conclusion regarding my perceptions and suggestions. If they did not change their decision by that time, I would leave. I could not be untrue to what I knew was the real leading of the Spirit for me and those for whose edification He had so graciously granted me the manifestation of His Spirit in the gift of teaching.

Six months later Jack found his way to my house. He

was a young brother whose friendship I cherished. *His House* was down to one member, he cried. Most of his friends were into carnal ways of living. Few spoke of Christ any more. What had gone wrong? Why hadn't I stayed to pull them through, he pleaded. Why had I left?

Unable to articulate the deep and almost overwhelming feelings painfully present in my heart, I simply gave him a long hug. I dared not venture a response lest the fragile dike inside of me burst, and then who knew what uncharitable things I might say in the emotion of the moment?

Grasshopper Christian or Free-Spirit Saint?

Many young Christians, especially those not raised in the Protestant churches of contemporary Christianity, have a very difficult time finding their place in the church. Their attempts to find their identity within the kingdom of God often appear bizarre to those unacquainted with the struggles they are undergoing. They are the chronic seekers of ecclesiology. They are accused of "just wanting to skim the cream off the assembly." In some cases this is true, yet in others, I wonder if there is not vision still waiting to be realized, a hope dimly burning, a dream which if brought to fruition might spark revival! Yet most are accused of wanting to benefit from only the church's most highly developed gifts or ministeries. These brethren are said to be unwilling to suffer the cost of assisting the church to develop the callings of God themselves. Some are described as "grasshopper Christians," idealistic fantacizers who are looking for the New Jerusalem here on earth. Often, even by Christians whose churches are badly in need of the Spirit's sovereign grace, the taunt is thrown at them, "You" will never find a perfect assembly—and if you do, don't join it or you'll ruin it." Are they really perfectionists? Or might some of them be prophets who are frustrated by the carnality pervading some denominational and non-denominational branches of the kingdom?

Reacting with carnal hostility, many of these younger believers wrongly deny the necessity for membership in a local church, as a defense against involvement in assemblies they visit which they cannot tolerate, let alone affirm. Referring to themselves as "free spirit saints" or "free-spirit Christians," they sometimes despair of ever finding a place where they can belong—where they can be free to love and be loved, to minister and be ministered to in an atmosphere of praise and rejoicing, of intimacy and spontaneity.

Ever since leaving *His House*, some of my Christian friends had accused me of being an incorrigible rebel, or unsubmissive upstart of this variety. During some periods of depression I often came to wonder if they weren't right. It appeared that my heart was growing full of perceptions concerning evangelical Christian life which I began to fear might smack of "accusing the brethren," thus manifesting pride and a lacking of mercy. One assembly after another was discounted as the church home to which Christ was leading me.

When I shared some personal struggles in the area of overcoming sin in my life with one pastor, he concluded that I needed the "baptism of the Holy Spirit" once again. This time, however, the minister was not in any way aligned with the neo-Pentecostal movement. He simply believed that heart holiness could be achieved through God's grace mediated to me through this experience. I wished he were right! Yet such an unscriptural view of sanctification gave me severe doubts about how effective he could be in facilitating any growth in me at all, for the Lord always seemed to bring about growth in my life very slowly. I would never meet this pastor's goal of instant sanctity by the laying on of hands.

Of course, I had done much to compound my own problems. One day in an assembly, a young minister involved in youth work asked for testimonies from the congregation. Being quite naive, I offered to share mine. In a brief manner, with as little detail as possible, I offered the fact that I had been gay and into drugs prior to my conversion. Then I praised the Lord for having saved me from this sinful life.

Oblivious to the fact that some Christians would sin against the Lord's injunction to "know no man after the flesh." I was unaware that I was changing the entire course of my Christianity that evening. Once I finished relating my conversion experience, I looked around the room for sympathetic understanding, even if not praise and rejoicing over what the Lord had done in my life. Dark scowls and shocked expressions convinced me in a flash that I had "blown it." I felt as if I wore the scarlet letter and wondered why the women didn't hug their children to their breasts and father's didn't guard their sons until I was escorted from the church. Apparently some pre-born-again lives of sin were "socially acceptable." Others, such as mine, obviously were "socially unacceptable." Who did I think I was, daring to speak openly in the assembly of having been redeemed from a life of such detestable sexual sin?

Ramifications of testifying about my past gay life extended into their elders' meetings and a counseling session in which I was definitely sinned against. The pastor informed me that his board had denied my request for the "right hand of fellowship" after merely hearing the word gay associated with my name. That had been enough for him, he confessed some years later. At that time he had wanted nothing more to do with such a "professing" Christian in his church. With 1,500 sheep in his flock he had enough problems. Who needed the words "homosexual" or "gay" floating around? Little did he realize, however, that statistically he already had at least 150 Christians from homosexual backgrounds in his congregation! Of course, with such an aura of homophobia (fear of homosexuality) in that assembly, how could you locate even one, to help minister to that person's specific spiritual needs?

During the entire period in which I was desperately seeking a church home, I had only a few close friends who were older saints and mature believers. Although they themselves were Christians I could admire and respect, they represented the thinking of two different evangelical traditions. Neither was denominationally oriented in the strictest and worst sense of the word. They loved the Lord, and their assemblies, yet they didn't attempt to force me into the congregations which they attended. Rather, they let me determine my own leading of the Spirit concerning this.

Beverley Blades was a woman of incredible gifts and callings who spoke of the Lord as if she had known Him forever. In my eyes she had! Saved many years, her understanding of God and her friendship with Jesus were as strong as the Rock of Gibraltar and found obvious expression in her life. Although this lovely woman in her forties had a flesh-and-blood family of her own, it took me years to figure out which children she and her husband, Joe, were raising were hers and which were foster children finding the love of the Lord under their roof. Never had I seen more highly developed pastoral and teaching gifts in any one woman. The children she counseled, spread across the land by now, number in the hundreds.

Because Bev did not live in Reno, but rather resided in Lake Tahoe, I seldom had the opportunity to speak with her face-to-face. Most often our fellowship was done over the phone, often at two or three o'clock in the morning! My loneliness, insecurity, and demanding personality probably convinced her that I was the Lord's special agent sent to her either as a "thorn in the flesh" to increase her already vast patience, or to precipitate that tribulation which brings about proven character.

This precious sister wasn't one to take God or His Word lightly. She would tolerate no complaining to Him (in prayer) or about Him (in fellowship). For those who loved the Lord (as she obviously did) His commands were not grievous. Only in Jesus' will could true liberation and freedom, joy and peace, be found. I must admit that often her views and mine didn't match. After a particularly lonely night or a severe temptation led to self-pity, I sometimes found her joy in the Lord's will incredible. Yet, daring to say anything about the supposed severity of the Lord's yoke I felt at one time or another would not be tolerated. It could even lead to the "ultimate option," as I called it. This consisted of Bev's quoting the Bible regarding the point under discussion and then adding the phrase "thus saith the Lord God." Then she would refuse to speak about the subject again. Under a heavy spirit of conviction, well buttressed by the relevant Scriptures she always gave, I never failed to repent.

John was dean of Sierra School of the Bible. I honestly didn't believe that anyone could have known Jesus as long nor as intimately as Beverly did, but I had to change my mind on that score when this brother entered my life. He had served in the ministry of teaching for probably as many years as I had lived. John, too, was to bear the unenviable task of being a phone friend, as he lived in Sparks. Most of my calls to him concerned points of doctrine which he seemed to understand and assist me on with ease. But sometimes other concerns expressed themselves as well.

"John," I confided almost in a whisper early one morning moments before the coming dawn, "I've really done it this time. I've sinned and I just can't live through the day without confessing it." Alert and attentive to this call for spiritual help, yet totally unconcerned about the particular nature of the evil perpetrated, this kind, scholarly, white-haired brother prayed with me until full repentance and fellowship with the Lord were a reality once more, and I could rest comfortably in the arms of Jesus again.

Even if I could not find a church home, I could at least revel in John and Beverly's friendship while I looked for it. The Lord had given me at least two believers with whom I could be totally honest about my successes and failures in the Christian life. Though churches as a group often rejected me (and me them), this brother and sister in Christ would not. Whenever things got rough, at least my "spiritual mother" and "spiritual father" were there. I could go to them for consolation and encouragement. Having no real local assembly, I couldn't have made it through without them.

Still, somewhere out there were Christians I could

relate to as a church. God, in the merciful provision of His grace, would either lead me to them or them to me. I prayed earnestly for involvement in just the right congregation. God had not brought me this far in the Christian life to leave me always in the threshold of His kingdom. Whether my vision of true Christianity, which I could not as yet articulate, could be found among real believers here on earth or not, I didn't know. If I had a "beam in my own eye" formulating negative perceptions of local churches in our area by it, the Lord would reveal this to me as well. Yet, always, though I could not verbalize the dream I had, I continued to hope I would experience its coming to fruition one day.

Until that time, I would continue on with a special involvement I had begun almost the night I was saved, and which had developed in leaps and bounds. Jesus had given us the command to go forth to all nations preaching the gospel message, and I had found my own very special way of doing it.

The Mission of Love

On many occasions I heard ministers preach on the importance of witnessing. In such sermons some pastors had a tendency to engender guilt in the hearts of their flocks, trying to manipulate them into sharing the gospel message. This was a sham and a travesty of the true spirit of evangelism. Although it may have succeeded in precipitating certain "desirable" actions in the lives of a few particularly impressionable souls for a time, it could never ultimately motivate them to a biblical understanding of and involvement in the church's true evangelical mission.

In much of this pulpit rhetoric regarding our responsibility to bear testimony to Christ, a truncated concept of witness is fostered. Emphasis is placed on the verbal, that is on the words said by the Christian to the unsaved man or woman. Yet a perceptive study of Christ's life and ministry, as well as a deep insight into basic communication principles, reveals that nine tenths of what we relate to others is conveyed nonverbally through the testimony of our lives. How often we maintain a zeal not in accordance with wisdom, by denying with our very actions the words of our mouths!

A third error preached in our assemblies is that true success in the evangelical enterprise consists of attracting great numbers of souls into the church. The top priority in this form of "evangelism" is quantity. Yet, to maintain such a viewpoint inevitably leads to a host of unscriptural practices and disastrous results. Our invitation becomes couched in humanistic terminology. Christ is often presented as a cosmic bromide for the ills of the world, a super Band-Aid for the wounds of past traumatic experiences or present situations with which an unsaved individual cannot cope. Repentance is underemphasized and those not looking for truth but rather for a way out of present difficulties are included in the mass of those said to be "saved." Ultimately, even when a synthetic gospel is preached, if the "evangelist" in this mind-set does not see results he imagines himself to be without the "gift," the "calling," or the "anointing" necessary to the task in which he is involved. He may even be rejected by himself, his missionary society, and his church as unfit for the Lord's work in this area. Untold numbers of missionaries have been broken in mind and spirit, both at home and on the foreign mission field, through adherence to this form of thinking.

Finally, the idolatry of materialism is sometimes fostered in the name of evangelism. Others are tempted to accept Christ on the grounds that their personal wealth can be enhanced, their societies and institutions benefited, and their lot in life bettered, if they give in to demands of the missionary. This form of unbiblical evangelistic endeavor is justified on the grounds that we have been exhorted to meet the physical needs of those we love. It is very subtle in its outworking and pagans quickly recognize and exploit its lucrative but fleshly potential. This can happen at the Gospel Mission down the street or in the economically depressed areas of the Third World nations.

Spirit-led evangelism, however, is always a life-style witness, bred of one's love for God and compassion for friends, neighbors, and enemies. It can never be imposed upon the believer by artifical means from without. It must be caused by the grace of God at work within the true believer. Indeed, nothing is more characteristic of the real Christian's life than the evangelical mission. The ultimate question is not how to motivate confessing Christians to the task of evangelism. It is merely how to keep false concepts of witnessing propagated by professing or misguided Christians, from replacing genuinely biblical ones in the missionary endeavors of the true church of Jesus Christ.

From the very first night that I met the Lord personally in my little apartment, on the very verge of suicide, I became possessed by an overwhelming love for God and my fellowman. This was not something I created, nor was it something I had to foster continually. Rather, it was simply a manifestation of the Holy Spirit's presence within me (Romans 5:5). Serving as a never-ending constraint upon my every thought and action, this newfound love compelled me to share Christ with others, for such simply is its nature: " . . . *God so loved the world, that He gave* His only begotten Son, that whoever believes in Him should not perish, but have eternal life" (John 3:16). The problem with most people (as it certainly had been with me prior to my salvation) is that they love others as they love themselves, in the worldly sense, whereas the true spirit of evangelism, which every true Christian receives, is to love others as they love themselves (and as God loves them) in the biblical sense. This, and this alone, is the only real motive to missionary activity.

A man cannot preach the resurrection until he has first been to Calvary. He cannot assess the true needs of others until he has first come to grips with his own, nor can he point others to the true meaning and purpose of life until he confronts, discovers, and accepts Him who is life's only real reason for being. Yet once this occurs, the fires of love which God the Holy Spirit enflames in his heart will cause the new Christian to burn with evangelistic zeal. Like Paul he will ask, "Lord, what would you have me do?" Jesus will respond, as He did so many years ago to the apostles, "Go therefore and make disciples of all the nations, baptizing them . . . teaching them to observe all that I have commanded you" (Matthew 28:19, 20).

Recognizing that true love must be expressed not only in word but in deed and truth, even the newest babe in Christ will express his love in action. He will not meet the needs of others as a form of manipulation by which he hopes to attract them to His Master. Rather, he will do so because he loves the unsaved with the same love with which he himself was loved even while he was yet a sinner in rebellion against the Lord. For this reason alone his lifestyle will validate his words.

While such a believer knows and can rest secure and be content in the fact that God's Word will never return to Him void, accomplishing His purposes in the lives of all those to whom it is sent, he will soon understand the truth of Jesus' words in Matthew 7:14: "For the gate is small, and the way is narrow that leads to life, and few are those who find it." He knows Christ's gospel will find a ready acceptance in the lives of fellow pilgrims here on earth. Yet he himself has experienced the fact that to become a follower of Jesus, means that all must be forsaken for the kingdom. He has counted the cost, hating everything, in comparison to His love for the Lord. This is not something most of those for whom his heart so burns to be saved will desire as well, "for many are called but few are chosen." He may cry to the Lord, as did the disciples while Christ was still on earth, "Are there few who are being saved?"

Yet, even at such times as these he will realize that he is not to be concerned with how many people respond to the invitation which he gives with his life. His concerns are not quantitative, they are qualitative. Jesus has already told him, "Not everyone who says to me Lord, Lord, will enter the kingdom of heaven, but he who does the will of my Father in heaven." His only duty is to see that those who do profess Christ through his ministry are also taught to obey all that Jesus has commanded us, and that they are prepared for the Master's imminent second coming by a life lived in the beauty of sanctification.

Thus his message will be authentic. He will challenge others to that holiness and righteousness without which no man shall see God. He will grieve over those who, like the rich young ruler, turn away, unwilling to pay the cost of true discipleship, but he will let them go. He recognizes that the Lord's commands are not burdensome to those whose hearts are filled with a real love for their Master. They will wish to please Him. They will respond to His desire. "If you love me, keep these commandments." They will not walk away when confronted by the lofty demands of their Savior.

In the final analysis, the missionary will be a man who becomes all things to all men that by the grace of God he might save some of them. Still, this identification with and empathy for a dying world will leave him untainted by its sin. He will be in it, but not of it. A clear distinction will always be apparent between his life and the lives of those to whom he gives himself. He is an ambassador of Christ, a stranger on earth, a messenger venturing into the kingdom of Satan, yet he realizes that "greater is he who is in you than he who is in the world." He worries not about his physical well-being, but rather his primary concern is with Him who can sentence to hell forever the bodies and souls of those who die unsaved.

Such indeed was the evangelistic mission and vision I received from Jesus soon after my salvation. Just as I did not even know the nature of the spiritual experience I had undergone at the time it occurred, I could not and did not back then articulate my desire to share Christ with others in the manner I do now. Yet, there it was, full bloom in my heart.

Initial rejection of Jesus as God by Steve, Vicki, Bill, Karen, and other college friends, led me to extend my range of relationships with fellow students. I shared Christ with professors, in most of my classes. Dr. Rants, my teacher of comparative religions, along with the rest, rejected my belief in Jesus as the only Lord and Savior of the world.

Philosophy classes began to yield bad grades. Always an excellent student, I had received a perfect 4.0 or "A" average in every philosophy class that I had taken. Now my philosophy papers were laced with cynical remarks and large red "Fs." Over and over, I was told that I was being unobjective regarding truth. What I should really be discussing, according to most of my professors, was truth as I understood it. How could it have been otherwise, I thought during those days. "The unspiritual mind cannot discern spiritual things." Still, it hurt me deeply when instructors inquired of me, as they frequently did, after my salvation, "You used to be such a good student. What happened to you?" While ingesting grass, hash, cocaine, and even acid, and on the very verge of suicide, my intellectual objectiveness had been applauded. Then I could say, "What is truth?" with the rest of the academicians. Now, I knew Him who alone is truth, and could only bear testimony to what little knowledge of Him and the revelation concerning His world I had. Thus I came to be regarded as somehow out of focus in my discernment of philosophical ideas. I was shrugged off by some of my professors as a Jesus freak who had dropped out of real, intellectual inquiry through adherence to primitive, orthodox, fundamental, evangelical Christianity.

Deciding that my relationship with Christ compelled me not restrict my witness to the intellectuals on campus, I began to take long walks in the evening, hoping to be led to someone who might accept His message. I would not give up my desire to share the Lord with professors and fellow students, but I would not limit my involvement to them alone. On one such sojourn downtown I found myself in the midst of this strange city in which God had chosen to save me.

Reno always seemed to be lit up like a carnival on the Fourth of July. White, red, orange, and green garish neon lights, which flashed sequentially, gave it an aura of plasticity and cheapness, of artificiality and commercialism. The city seemed to stand out in stark ugly contrast to the beautiful snow-capped mountains in whose valley it rested. Sauntering down "The Strip," I found myself walking on maroon indoor-outdoor carpeting stretched almost to the curb. Casino after casino (one eleven stories high) encompassed me on both sides of Virginia Street, making me feel, somehow, gripped in the clutch of Satan. Harrah's, Harold's, The Money Tree, The Mapes—on and on they went, disappearing farther down beyond the Truckee River. Yes, I mused, Reno and Las Vegas are truly twin cities of sin, the Sodoms and Gomorrahs of our day. How ironic it was to be living in a city, where as a newborn Christian people came as tourists to do nothing more than indulge themselves in gambling, drinking, viewing half-naked women in floor shows, and trying to find some happiness in this all, which would convince them that life wasn't so bad after all.

Growing increasingly depressed, I peered into the open doors of the casinos. Fashionably dressed middle-aged visitors tugged on slot machines, as other excited patrons tossed dice at huge "craps" tables nearby. "Twenty-one" dealers dealt cards with a precision that appeared almost mechanical. Roulette wheels spun endlessly as Keno boards flashed numbers at men and women, soon to convert them into "wins" or "losses" on the little cards they circled with large black crayons. Incredibly ornate bars, some so long I couldn't even see the far end of them, lined the walls. Young bar boys ran to and fro attempting to keep them well stocked with the liquor that seemed to flow like water. Thousands of people ordered their drink's so fast I couldn't imagine how the bartenders could keep up with them.

Turning a corner now (left onto sixth street), I observed wedding chapels with artificial glowing facades attempting to add a note of joy to a second, third, or fourth marriage, all the while bearing testimony to the fragility of the secular marriage bonds they validated. How many shattered dreams had young men and women brought here for repairs, I wondered? How many hopes and aspirations had commenced here? How many people ultimately realized that what they really sought could not be found in these pagan temples offering nothing more than cohabitation with legal and perhaps the appearance of ecclesiastical approval? No, it wasn't strange, I concluded, that the marriage mecca of the world should be its divorce capital as well. Unions bred in such an atmosphere seemed doomed to dissolution from the start.

Later on, passing once more through the endless maze of glittering pleasure palaces, I saw a prostitute plying her trade on the corner. Against the First National Bank building some young hippies dealt grass with furtive glances for the presence of police, their knapsacks lined up against the bottom of the edifice in a neat row. Long-haired and clad in sandals (or with no shoes at all), they sought lodging for the night in one crash pad or another.

Then the thought exploded into my consciousness like a thunderbolt out of the clouds of gloom now present there. I knew that security guards and pit bosses observed every one of the thousands of casino patrons with an expert eye. Anyone daring to violate the unwritten rules of the casino were doomed to immediate expulsion. I couldn't witness as "in the world but not of it" within their confines, but I could invite one or two of these young hippies home with me for a hot meal, a night's lodging, and whatever ministry Jesus would point out to me could be done for them!

But should I risk it? The cost seemed incredibly high. What if I was thought to be cruising? I could easily be beaten to death if one of the young "street people" misunderstood my intentions. Who knew what drug they might be on, and what effects it would produce not only in their lives but in mine as well? I had to get alone and pray this one through.

Leaning against the cement buttress of the bridge over the Truckee River (off which divorced couples traditionally throw their discarded wedding rings), I shared my thoughts and feelings with the Lord. "Jesus, You told us to go forth preaching Your gospel message, but I'm afraid," I said.

"Fear not he who can kill the body. Rather, fear him who can sentence the body and soul to hell," Jesus replied. Then He added one of His clinchers, always sure to make me feel ridiculous at my self-protective nature. "Perfect love casts out fear. I have done away with your fear of me. Isn't it in accord with love that you should help end others' fear of Me as well?"

On and on went the dialogue until the Lord brought to light the true nature of the problem with which I was struggling. It was pride, sure and simple. That subtle enemy lay even deeper than the superficial fear I had originally felt. I was not familiar with street people. My wealthy foster parents had given Chip and me everything we needed on a physical level. Monastic training followed by college studies made me feel somehow superior to those ragged youths back by the bank. I was prejudiced against them, believing that their lack of formal education and poverty was bred of rebellion. They seemed egotistical and hell-bent for destruction. Why should I be the one to risk my life for them?

The Holy Spirit never fails to bring the right text to life in my heart at such times. "Love your enemies. Do good to those who hate you and despitefully use you," He commanded. "Either My word finds practical application in your life, or you must stop professing to be a Christian. Stop quenching and grieving Me. What if I had refused to come to you that night your own depravity and sinfulness overwhelmed you? You say that you love Me. You say that I have given you a love for others, and you are right. I have. Let it flow from the depths of your heart. It will soon override your pride and fear. Trust Me, for I am with you always. Nothing can happen in your life that I do not allow. I will use whatever circumstances and situations emerge to benefit you and others in ways you cannot even imagine now."

Finally, the Lord brought to my mind the words of Francis Schaeffer in his book, *The Church at the End of the Twentieth Century.* Here the biblical concepts which the Lord Himself had shared with me earlier found an exposition in life that further compelled me to the mission of love to which He was calling me. I couldn't deny their application that night:

There is a different kind of unantiseptic situation. How

many times have you taken a drug user into your home? Sure it is a danger to your family, you must be careful. But have you ever risked it? If you don't risk it, what are you talking about the drug problem for, if in the name of Christ you have not tried to help somebody in this horrible situation!

If you have never done any of these things or things of this nature, if you have been married for years and years and had a home (*or even a room*) and none of this has ever occurred, if you have been quiet especially as our culture is crumbling about us, if this is so, do you really believe that people are going to hell? And if you really believe that, how can you stand and say, "I have never paid the price to open my living place and do the things I can do"?

I have a question in my mind about us as evangelicals. We fight the liberals when they say there is no hell. But do we really believe people are going to hell?

It is not only at L'Abri, in the Alps, where this has meaning. When I was a pastor, I knew what it meant to go down to the nightclubs at night and fish the drunks out at three or four o'clock in the morning and take them to their homes. Do you?

. . . this is the way community begins. There is no other way. Everything else is false if it is further away than this.

The Bible says we are to give out cups of cold water. How many have we ever given out to the long-haired and barefooted boys? Don't try to get your church to begin, if you haven't begun it for yourself.

A revolution is coming and is here. If we don't have the courage in Jesus Christ to take a chance of getting kicked out of our churches and being ostracized today, what are we going to do when the revolution comes in force? If we don't have the courage to open our homes and begin to enter these things into the churches, slowly begin to make the changes that can be brought about . . . then don't be concerned about having courage when the pressure comes.

We send martyrs off to the end of the earth and say go ahead and die for Jesus Christ. Why not here at home?

There was no mistaking it. The Lord, both directly through His Word, and then through the words of one of His servants, was giving me a call to go back to that street corner and invite one or two of the hippies I had seen to my home for the night. No force in the universe could have caused me to pass up those rebellious youths on my way back home to my apartment. Whatever happened from here on in was Jesus' concern and not mine. Andrew Murray's affirmation served as a final means of grace to my trembling heart. "The Lord is fully capable of taking complete responsibility for the life which is totally yielded to Him," he had said.

Finding my way through a throng of wealthy and respectable fashionably dressed sinners who tottered drunkenly out of the casinos in this now very late hour of the night, I made my way back to the little group of hippies on the corner by the bank. Approaching them slowly, I asked Jesus for just the right opening words. In a moment He gave them to me. "I am a Christian," I said to two young guys obviously thoroughly chilled by the almost freezing night winds that had sprung up. "Would either of you want to come home with me and share the Lord's house for the night? I only live six blocks away."

Mike and Jim made me feel almost sheepish as they said with a politeness I never expected, "Sure, man, we're really cold. Hey, thanks a lot." Grabbing their backpacks and sleeping bags, they followed me the few blocks to my apartment, obviously most grateful for the invitation.

My first two guests were the beginning of a style of evangelism that was to encompass the entire next three years of my life. Mike and Jim were classical Street

People who informed me over a steaming cup of coffee that they were doing their own thing. Though hostile to any form of authority they had ever encountered, they were, nevertheless, open, friendly, and even gentle toward those who made no demands upon them.

Very sensitive toward my initial anxiety over having brought two young rebels home with me, both guys took turns in alleviating whatever fears I might have had. They assured me that they were not carrying grass. Each of them had been befriended by Christians many times in the past. Their knowledge of Jesus freaks, as they called the Christians they had met, was extensive. Though neither of them would have agreed to attend a church to listen to a presentation of the gospel message in its pews, their questions regarding Jesus poured forth from them in my home like a river at flood tide overflowing its banks.

They leveled the classical charges against the churches of our time at me along with other searing questions. "Aren't Sunday morning church-goers, hypocrites? "Don't most preachers really look more toward a man's wallet than to the needs of his heart? How come most congregations are so cold?" they demanded. Inevitably their accusations focused on past encounters they had experienced with parents, relatives, and friends who had been harsh purveyors of a law morality, or churches in which they had been raised which attempted to incorporate them into an ecclesiastical system while paying little attention to their perceptions, feelings, or emotional needs.

During the early morning hours before dawn, I fried eggs, poured water into a large pan so they could bathe their blistered feet, poured coffee, and finally ended up darning ripped jeans, as Mike and Jim bared their souls, expressing a desire to be heard—which often left little opening for verbal response. Though I knew that much of what they were saying was nothing more than an attempted justification of the lifestyle they had chosen, to avoid real responsibility, I offered no rebuke to their hostility nor any criticism of their blatant unwillingness to follow Christ.

Whenever I could, I corrected their misconceptions of Christianity as equated with church attendance and adherence to ritual. I clarified their thinking regarding the person and work of Jesus as Lord and Savior. I pointed to the Bible as the one true locus of all earthly authority, and affirmed their belief that much congregational discipline simply "provoked unto anger". Financial considerations were important, but often overemphasized, I agreed, and I couldn't understand either why more involvement with Christians could not take place in informal settings such as the one in which we were now involved.

Yet, always, I brought the responsibility for the sinful lives of premarital sex, involvement in drugs, and willful rebellion back to both young men placing it squarely on their shoulders. Just because many people in the church did not live lives consistent with the desires of God did not mean that Mike and Jim were justified in joining the ranks of such hypocrites as well. Who knew what type of suffering Mike and Jim would have to bear, even at the hands of those already professing Christ, once they themselves repented. But if they were going to be honest with Jesus, they would have to bear reproach, helping to correct such abuses, rather than using them as a ready excuse to discount the true gospel of the Lord. They both agreed with this logic, yet neither of them wished to live a true Christian life of faith in God and obedience to the Lord.

As dawn finally broke, I found myself trying to get some sleep on the floor so that Mike could have my bed. He had no sleeping bag and seemed to be tortured with a bad cold, perhaps he even had pneumonia. Though he slept well into the coming day, both Mike and Jim had left by the time I arose. My encounter with them was only a memory the following afternoon as I wandered in a lethargic state toward the now empty coffee pot. Only one evidence of their having stayed with me the previous night remained. The note read:

Dear Brother,

Thanks for the night. I ain't gonna accept Jesus just cause you said I should, but you really got to me, especially about how all those prophecies in the first part of the Bible came true in Jesus' life, and about how I couldn't blame doing my thing on hypocrites who call themselves Christians, but are really playing a game with Christ. Who knows? maybe someday I'll get saved like you, and if so I want to talk to people about God just like you do.

Hope you get money to buy more coffee. If others who come drink as much as we did, you'll never keep up. Keep the faith.

Mike.

P.S. You sure ain't one of them hypocrites in the church. You tell it like it is and live it to!

Tears poured from my eyes in such a ready stream that I barely made out the P.S. "Thank you, Jesus," I cried. "Thank you, Lord, for giving me the privilege of sharing your love with those kids. I know You don't need any of us, but that You do give us the joy of being used. Please, Jesus," I added, "use me again like that." I knew after reading that note, however, that my request to share Jesus' love with street people was unnecessary. The future was inevitable now. My one desire—to share the love of the Lord with transients—would become a reality!

Reno, I soon learned from other young guests who stayed a night with me on Lake Street, lay right on the main artery between Los Angeles, San Francisco, Salt Lake City, and points east. Virtually every street person who traveled across country passed through its city limits. There was no emergency center where they could find food and lodging. Many who entered the town had been beaten on the highway or had had their packs stolen by fellow travelers. Some were runaways, while others were ex-felons or con artists. Still others were high school or college students, lured to the road by the hope of adventure. I was in a perfect position to share Christ in word and action with thousands of transient young people. And for the following months and years that's just what I did.

I doubt that there's any other way in which I could have received a better orientation to the ways and manners of such a broad spectrum of society as I encountered through this ministry. Glen, a Buddhist, fell down almost the entire flight of stairs leading to my apartment because he was suffering from the effects of a hunger strike he had begun three months earlier. He explained to me that he was trying to purge his system of the infectious poisionous pesticides from canned foods he had eaten in earlier years. Betty claimed to be a witch, offering spells and incantations to other young people for free. "Blue" spent his night in my home on speed, chattering away like a monkey, almost oblivious to what he said, once it was out of his mouth. Larry lived most of the year in a cave in Southern California, while Gerry spent his life in a tree house he had built as a home when he was not traveling. Dick was an English professor at an Eastern college and had a Master's degree. And Frank was a Christian himself, passing through Reno on his way back to a ministry in Fresno, California.

None of these people who found their way to my apartment ever accepted the Lord on the spot, yet night after night I would find a note saying that one of them or another had come to see Jesus in an entirely new perspective, not as Someone who was against them because of their sin, but as a Person who was with them against their sin. Almost all of my street people had heard John 3:16 over and over. Few, if any, could quote the following verse prior to the evening they spent with me. "For God did not send the Son into the world to judge the world; but that the world should be saved through Him." The one thing which struck these youngsters more than anything else was the affirmative spirit of the gospel, and the genuine manner in which it was presented. If this only was accomplished, I thought, my time had certainly been well spent. Jesus never says to us, "Well done, good, faithful, *and successful* servant." For success is not our primary concern—love is. Rather, He says simply, "Well done, good and faithful servant," and I had no doubt He was saying this to me, whether I saw conversions or not.

We Are the Church!

The Mission of Love was definitely growing! In the year since I had begun to offer street people a night's lodging in Jesus' name, almost a thousand young men and women had accepted my invitation! I was becoming known in Reno as a person to whom various agencies could refer transients for a night. Calls began to come from the Red Cross, the Crisis Call Center, the Teenage Line for Crisis, the Salvation Army, the Gospel Mission, and from Christians all over the city, asking me if I would help this person or that one find a place to stay, a job, a hot meal, or a friend to talk to in a difficult period of their lives.

Fellow believers began to take an interest in the work. I found that many gifted young people whose gifts were being overlooked or ignored in their own assemblies really wanted to be of service to the Lord. One by one they came—my old friend, Nan, who had first invited me to *His House;* Barry, a black ex-gay Christian with much time on his hands; Tom, a brother who enjoyed street witnessing more than anyone I had ever met; and Bob, who had known the Lord since he was a young child.

It soon became obvious to me that the small one-bedroom apartment in which I lived was inadequate for the ministry into which the Lord had led me. I needed a residence that could accommodate not only the street people who were staying with me each night, but also a group of young brothers who had devoted themselves to the Lord's ministry in which we were engaged. My individual personal evangelism, and my ministry to already saved Christians who wanted to help in the work, was growing into a fellowship of believers who were touching the lives of young people across the United States and Canada as they stayed with us for one night in Reno.

In answer to our prayers, a four-bedroom house on Denslowe Drive was secured and four brothers moved in.

We were confident that God would continue not only to bless the Mission of Love, but that He would also facilitate our own growth and Christian maturity through communal living. Though we all came from diverse denominational backgrounds, that made little difference to us back then. We were cemented into a bond of unity by our relationship to Jesus and our evangelistic zeal. Our intention was to be a fellowship of believers and nothing more.

The Mission of Love continued on for another year, with brothers combing the streets of Reno for young people in need of a place to stay. Some of us sang songs and prayed for the city as we walked through its transient routes ever alert for the backpack or sleeping bag that would indicate a street person who might enjoy the night as our guest.

Others took their cars to the truck stop on the east side of town. There they alerted hitchhikers—asleep by the side of the road, cold and sick sometimes—that there was a warm shower, a hot meal, and a congenial place to talk and rest waiting for them at the Mission of Love.

The police began to take notice of what we were doing and brought needy individuals to us. Often they referred stranded families to us as well. Once they brought us a family of twelve, complete with grandmother and grandfather, who had been sleeping in the men's room of a wayside rest stop. The grandfather was blind and his progeny smelled deeply of smoke from the small campfires around which they had been huddling for a little warmth in the night.

Many times those who had lost their money in the casinos found themselves without enough cash to buy a bus ticket to return home to another city or state. While they raised the funds, our home became theirs as well.

Once I was put in charge of a black six-year-old youngster from Los Angeles, whose mother had lost a large sum of money in one of the clubs. As we waited together outside the casino for his mother to arrange her finances with the manager, if she could, my little charge began a bizarre charade with passersby. Much to my horror, he picked up a cigarette stub, placed it in his mouth, cocked his arm on his hip, and told everyone in the vicinity that he was a pimp, looking for "duckets" (money). I had to seat him on the curb firmly to avoid further antics.

After a year of this type of ministry, one Sunday evening I found myself stirring a large kettle of chocolate with Nan, as my brothers and sisters in the Lord played outside in the snow which thickly carpeted the entire city. I felt content. My life was filled with friends and fellow believers, and I was somehow expecting even better things in the future, although I had no idea what these might be.

Shortly after my snow-covered "family" returned inside to empty the steaming cups of cocoa we poured, we found ourselves involved in a life-changing discussion. Not one of us was aware that evening where the conversation would lead or what changes in our lives would result from it.

It was Nan, as usual, who shattered the peace of that tranquil living room with nothing more than an affirmation, but it was an affirmation born out of a deep insight into the working of the Holy Spirit in our midst. "You know, Kev," she began. "You are my pastor and this is my church." Not even giving me time to catch my breath, she continued, "This is the kind of fellowship that pleases the Lord! Why don't we just make it official? Isn't it obvious that this is where God has been leading us to all along? Let's stop looking for the special church in which He wants us, and start recognizing that we are the church He has created!"

"What!" I exclaimed. "Nan, you couldn't be right about this one. We're a fellowship, not a church. I've only been saved a few years. I've never even been to Bible school, and who would ever think of an ex-gay Christian becoming a pastor!" With that series of rationalizations, I knew beyond a doubt that I had resolved the issue once and for all—but it was soon clear that I was wrong once again.

"Look," Nan argued, "pastor-teacher is a gift, not an office, and you have that calling. Many churches in Acts were established without elders being appointed first. In fact," she continued, "elders were appointed last. And as far as our being a fellowship and not a church, how can you say that with certainty?" On and on she went finally arriving at the subject of my pre-conversion lifestyle. "You are the one who told us that we are to know no man after the flesh, and that you are upset at the sin of people who do. You yourself have taken 1 Corinthians 6:9-11 as a life motto. Doesn't it say that some of you *were* homosexuals *before meeting Christ* and that you have been washed, justified, and sanctified in the name of the Lord Jesus Christ and in the Spirit of our God?"

Before I could get a word out of my mouth, Barry joined in. "Look, Kev, it's not that we're just rebels expressing dissatisfaction with the institutionalized churches that we've seen. Man, we'd run to the right one if we could find it. It's just that, well, you know what we're looking for, and none of us have been able to discover it." Looking down at the floor, almost embarrassed, he added, "Nowhere, that is, except here!"

It was no use. Every defense I made against the impossible idea was refuted directly from the Word. As far as the entire fellowship was concerned, they were committed and ready to affirm what the Lord was doing in their hearts. And what they said He was doing was forming them into a church, not just a fellowship any longer.

For three months following that Sunday evening, I wrestled with the Lord about what He had done that night. My underlying insecurity and poor self-image tortured me beyond belief. Why, I pleaded with God, did everyone force me into the position of a leader, when my real desire was to follow, to rest securely in the leadership gifts He gave to others? If only I could find the right assembly in Reno, I told the Lord, if only I could meet someone who had a similar vision and was willing and able to lead, I could then become a part of what He had done in them. I could be a member of a new church without having to lead. Day after day, week after week, month after month, I agonized with the seriousness of assuming a pastoral role—considering my scarred background. Finally, I could stand it no longer.

Long into the night I prayed for the Lord to persuade me, or put me into a hospital, or even to take me away from the group in Reno, if I should not become their pastor. Searching the Word I hoped to be disqualified from the task by some new scriptural revelation. This did not occur. In the early hours of the breaking dawn, I acquiesced to the Lord's will and accepted the call.

However, prior to informing the group about my decision, I decided to devote myself to a period of Bible study. Paul told us to be imitators of him, even as he was of Christ, so I turned to my favorite epistle, 2 Corinthians, to see if the Lord would give me any special instructions or admonitions regarding my call to the pastorate. The first three chapters held little of special interests to me that night. But arriving at chapter four, verse 1, the gold letters I had come to associate with the Holy Spirit's illumination flashed once more on the background of my mind, and they said:

> Therefore, since we have this ministry, as we received mercy, we do not lose heart, but we have renounced the things hidden because of shame, not walking in craftiness or adulterating the word of God, but by the manifestation of truth commending ourselves to every man's conscience in the sight of God.

Those words were to become the key channel of grace for me in my ministry during the next several years and have remained the primary scriptural description of what I believe God is doing in my ministry. So long as I remained true to the ideal they presented, I knew that Jesus would bring our little community through all the trials and struggles it would encounter, at least insofar as its pastoral service was concerned.

Although our little group did not have an exact formula or absolute blueprint for what they felt our church should be like that didn't matter to us. Various encounters in local congregations had taught us some things which must be avoided. The Bible contained the positives, and the Holy Spirit would quicken them to our hearts in the course of time. We believed that the church was like a person—it must grow and mature through the callings, gifts, and leading of God presented to it in the trials, victories, struggles and triumphs of everday life.

Initially, we did begin our serach for God's will as an assembly through reading Dr. Schaeffer's *The Church at the End of the Twentieth Century*. We felt that this book was scriptural and concentrated on the forms and freedoms for the church presented in the Bible. In this work, Schaeffer presents nine essentials of an orthodox biblical Christian congregation:

1. Churches should be made up of Christians but these churches have no direct connection with a church building.
2. Congregations should meet together in a special way on the first day of the week.
3. Church officers (elders) should be given responsibility for the local churches.
4. Deacons should be responsible for the members of the church in the area of material things.
5. The community of faith should take discipline seriously.
6. Specific biblical qualifications are given for elders and deacons.
7. The church also exists on a larger than local church basis.
8. The two sacraments of baptism and the Lord's Supper are to be practiced.
9. Anything the New Testament does not command in regard to church form is a freedom to be exercized under the leadership of the Holy Spirit for that particular time and place.

Agreeing on these points, we also affirmed that orthodoxy of doctrine must parallel orthodoxy of love or community. We accepted Tillich's statement that "the truth without love is not truth at all, and love without the truth isn't love at all" (*The New Being*). Our assembly would always attempt to maintain both in proper balance.

We considered several other components of the scripturally functioning church as imperative even in the church's initial stages. Radical discipleship headed the list. Each person was to maintain a spiritual walk with the Lord in which Jesus was his or her first love. Our community would be charismatic, with everyone free to use the gifts in the assembly so long as the injunctions of 1 Corinthians 12 and 14 were observed. We affirmed the house church concept as the Lord's leading for us. We felt that this expressed the best form of stewardship over our finances and fostered an informal atmosphere which we greatly appreciated. A nonverbal assumption seemed to be that if the assembly grew too large to function comfortably in one home, we would split and form another house church rather than meeting in a larger building. We agreed that women were to be veiled in accordance with 1 Corinthians 11. This would express their equality of dignity but distinction of role in the church and symbolize their spirit of submission to Christ and to their husbands.

For the next year our assembly continued its outreach on the streets. Our move to a fifteen-room abandoned mansion on Ralston Street was precipitated by thirteen professions of faith made by street people to whom we ministered and who believed that the Lord was leading them to stay with us for discipleship. More and more young men and women were discovering and reveling in the presence of Jesus in our midst. Once again the Lord called us to abandon our comfortable home and find a larger one.

The proud old mansion almost seemed to welcome us with hope in its sagging heart as we explored its maze of rooms and corridors. Once the private residence of a casino owner, it had been forsaken to the winds of time and circumstance. The present owners were lawyers who rented to us on an as-is basis for four hundred dollars a month. Any repairs, plus the two hundred dollar a month fuel bill, must be paid as well by the brothers who would reside there.

Perhaps the most intriguing single component of the large structure was its huge sunken tub in the first-floor bathroom. Of course to us it was to become a baptistry where baptisms by immersion could be easily facilitated. We laughed with delight as we noted its three-foot depth. Perhaps we were the only house church in the nation with such an exquisite place of baptism right under our roof.

We could not afford repairs of substantial nature. However, a coat of paint here and a new piece of carpeting there made the the big house more than livable. Its eight bedrooms would make each of our guests feel safe and comfortable, for they could each have one of their own.

Finding my way into a large first-floor room I knew immediately would serve as my office, I dropped to my knees and lifted my arms high in the air. "Thank you, Jesus," I prayed, "for providing this unbelievable home for your friends and enemies. Lord," I continued, "please don't ever let this house be a reproach to Your name. Please fill it with the presence of Your Spirit, and let each of us brothers who reside here grow in conformity to Your character living in this, Your gift to us, in Jesus' name."

For another year the virtual onslaught of street people kept us so busy that we seldom had time to relax or enjoy ourselves. Our evangelism was an extensive enterprise. Often I shared Christ with hitchhikers from 12:00 noon until four o'clock in the morning. Brothers and sisters cooked, drove newly arrived guests to one appointment or another in the city, and played a never-ending series of Christian albums for them on the stereo in the living room. Often we had 26 people a night staying with us now, as diverse in their theological and cultural backgrounds as those at my original apartment on Lake Street had been.

One night far into the freezing Nevada winter, a crisis developed which none of us could handle. The electrical system of the mansion had been precariously pieced together through the years. Each time a blizzard arose, house ministry members found themselves groping in the dark for candles and flashlights until sooner or later—usually in twenty minutes or so—the lights would come back on and the electricity would function properly once again. This time, however, we knew that the wiring in the kitchen was out for good, and we certainly didn't have the money to call an electrician.

Meeting together in the dining room, the entire church, which was assembled for a Tuesday night Bible study, considered alternatives. No one could come up with a satisfactory solution to our problem. But something obviously had to be done. If the electricity stayed off much longer, the pipes would freeze and break, making the old mansion no longer habitable. Finally I decided to call the landlord, who was not a very friendly man, and see if he would allow us to call a serviceman.

His phone rang time and time again but there was no answer. Just as I decided to hang up and try again later, a gruff voice boomed over the line, "Hello. What do you want?" Explaining my difficult dilemma brought no positive response or sympathetic offer of help from Zeke.

"You guys took the house on an as-is basis," he yelled, "and it's up to you to see that it's kept in the same shape as when you leased it. If you let those pipes freeze, you've had it." The phone clicked in my ear, while I simply stood there too shocked to replace the receiver on the hook.

Returning to the church, gathered around a little oil lamp in the now much colder dining room, I related Zeke's response to my plea for assistance in our crisis. They were crestfallen, having prayed that the Lord would intervene in our behalf during my negotiations with the landlord. Finally, however, Nan spoke up. "Of course," she said. "Praise the Lord in all things. Praise! Praise!" We all stared at her, confident that this time she had really "flipped out." But her response to our upraised eyebrows proved that once again her heart was open wide to the Holy Spirit's leading. Someone reached for a guitar and the entire little band of disciples began singing songs of rejoicing to their Savior, oblivious to the falling temperature in the room.

Twenty minutes later, the phone rang. It was Zeke. "Listen, Kev," he said. "I've been really lousy to you guys and you've been really straight with me. Go ahead and call the electrician. I'll pay for it myself, and by the way," he added, "I want to lower your rent fifty dollars a month!"

"Oh, me of little faith," I moaned as I turned from the phone, "How could I have given up hope!"

The entire church simply nodded approvingly when I told them what had transpired. They knew already somehow that their praises had been heard by the Lord. Their joyful response simply was to continue singing their love to Him far into the night, even after the power had been restored. Over and over again we saw Jesus perform similar miracles, either for ourselves directly or for our street people.

Roy was the recipient of God's next miraculous intervention. He was fifteen years old and as rebellious as they come. Only one difference seemed to separate him from the other transients we had had as visitors recently. Somehow, he seemed to be saved. Of course he professed Christ as Lord and Savior. Practially all of our guests did. But we seldom bore witness to such professions in our hearts, and this teenager had given me a full bag of "whites" on entering the Lord's house due to our policy of turning away any young person unwilling to surrender his drugs, yet seeking help at our door.

Two weeks after Roy arrived he decided that he no longer wanted to stay with us for discipleship. No amount of conversing with him could change his mind. He was going to Las Vegas and then on south, perhaps to the Mardi Gras in Louisiana. With a final slam of the huge front door he was gone forever, or was he?

Each brother prayed for Roy upon his departure. We felt strongly that he was really headed for trouble unless God intervened in his life in some unexpected manner. Yet as nighttime arrived and he did not return, our minds focused on other responsibilities in the ministry that needed attention. We simply commended Roy to the care of the Lord and to His Word.

A knock at the door revealed a mournful pair of dark blue eyes and a long shock of blond hair that could only be Roy's! "Praise God!" I shouted, hugging him intermittently as I danced around the newly returned prodigal son. "What happened to you?" I finally managed to inquire as brothers and sisters surrounded

Roy, filled with the belief that Jesus had worked some miracle to accomplish his return.

"You aren't going to believe this," Roy said, "but I was on my way to Vegas, and was really halfway there when nightfall set in. I was cold and really began to get scared when no cars came in either direction for some time. I was freezing, man, and I might have died, but for something you told me, Kev. After I was sure I wasn't going to get a ride, I thought of what you said about Jesus always being with us, even when we rebel against Him—how He's not against us because of our sins but with us against our sins, you know.

"Well, I decided to pray," Roy continued. "I was honest with God just like you told me to be. I said, 'Lord, if You want me to go back to that ministry, You're going to have to bring me back there because I ain't going.' But I added, 'If You give me a ride back I'll know that's where You want me to be and I'll give in and do what You want me to do.' About ten minutes later I saw lights on the opposite side of the highway from the shoulder of the road I was on, so I ran to the other side and thumbed a ride. Wouldn't you know it. It was the Baptist pastor from Fallen and he brought me right here to the steps of the ministry, far out of his way, while talking about Jesus just like you guys do all the way!"

In spite of such miraculous occurrences as those which Roy and others could relate after having spent some time at the house ministry, we knew that too much of our time was being spent in evangelism. As the year wore on we saw a "praise-the-Lord-and-pass-the-potatoes" attitude develop among our young guests that made us wonder if we were not sometimes actually contributing to their irrational lifestyles by being such ready sources of physical comfort. Often now our own church was being neglected to meet the needs of others. We knew that we had to meet the real needs of the local assembly first if we were to have anything to share with those who came from outside seeking help. The whopping one-thousand-dollar-a-month bills were depleting our financial resources, and we believed that the Lord was calling us to end the Mission of Love giving more time and attention to the needs of the church.

We were right about the Mission of Love. After the lease expired we were three thousand dollars in debt for our ministry to Reno area transients. During the entire period in which we had washed their feet in love, in Jesus' name, the work had been supported by the brothers living in the house ministry and the church Christ had founded in our midst. We felt that we should pay this debt off completely to avoid giving a bad stewardship testimony to those to whom we owed money.

So we moved our headquarters across the street from the old Ralston Street Manor and turned our attention to working off our debt as we grew together in the Lord developing new ministries and outreaches. Some of the questions which arose during this period to challenge the little fellowship were: (1) How do we relate to those who differ with us in doctrine? (2) What are the qualifications for elders? (3) How do we properly apply the disciplinary process given in Matthew 18? (4) How should spiritual gifts function properly in the assembly. Aside from these "practical" matters our assembly considered such doctrinal questions as the following: (1) Is there really a pretribulational rapture? (2) Are the carnal Christian teachings of some congregations scriptural? (3) How does the Lord deal with us in the process of sanctification? (4) Is

Arminianism or Calvinism a truer assessment of the
Spirit of God's revelation as given in the Bible?

Finally after a year on Bell Street, our small two-
bedroom home was becoming cramped once more. Our
house church fellowship began to pray for a permanent
place of residence. In only a month those petitions had
been heard and answered by God. One of the western
Mennonite Conferences helped us purchase a four-
bedroom home, with a large living room, only three
blocks from the University of Nevada. Here our congregation could grow, unhampered by the acute housing
shortage in Reno which necessitated almost yearly leases
at high monthly rent payments.

New ministries and outreaches were begun, the most
controversial of which was the ex-gay ministry. Local
newspapers featured articles on the ex-homosexual
Christian who had begun to share the message of a new
life in Christ to gays throughout the northern Nevada
area. *Sounds of Joy,* an internationally broadcast
synidcated radio program, invited me to speak my
message from God on their show. An article entitled "A
Pastoral Response to Homosexuality" was published in
the *Gospel Herald* and the *Mennonite Brethren Herald.*
Tracts, such as "Created to Glorify God" and "Such
Were Some of You," were published by Herald Press in
Scottdale, Pennsylvania. Our newly established homosexual hotline, and ex-gay intervention team ministries
were launched, and a newsletter to gays and saved men and
women who were once homosexual was published.

God richly blessed our outreach in this area. Jeff, a
young premed student in Illinois, received one of our
newsletters and took us up on our invitation to visit the
house church for a week. This short visit turned into

months as our new baby brother received Christ, transferred his college work to a university here, and remained with us to grow in his new relationship with Jesus. Mark, once a developer of the Metropolitan Community Church in Fresno, California, met our team at a Mennonite Brethren-hosted conference on homosexuality at the Biblical Seminary there and asked the Lord into his heart. After a weekend visit to Reno, we knew he was serious about living a lifestyle glorifying to his Savior.

Keith, a young high school honors student, who was ex-gay, joined us with the consent of his pastor, and realized real victory in his life while surrounded by those who understood and could relate to his problems out of firsthand experience.

Other brothers and sisters from the fellowship discovered different avenues of service to the Lord. Each Saturday they drove off to Carson City for a visit with fellow Christians in prison. An extensive correspondence ministry developed to prisoners throughout the United States and Canada. Hopes for an ex-felon post-release center grew in their hearts.

New young Christians searching for a radical discipleship community have joined us both singly and in pairs. Terry and Maria and Rick and Rhonda planned their weddings which were the first we had solemnized in our assembly. Although some past members were called by the Lord to new endeavors elsewhere in His kingdom, the little house church continues their witness to Jesus, inviting persons—whatever their background—to find wholeness and joy in Him and to find fellowship with other believers.

As for myself, my new life in Christ has not been easy.

God hasn't given me a wife and children and sometimes I still am severely tempted. Sometimes even Christians are shocked at the possibility of God turning a homosexual into an ex-gay Christian. But I don't mind.

I know the freedom and the liberation of living a life in accordance with the will of Jesus. I know what it is like to have Him control my life instead of being driven by some other force. I know the truth of what someone told me shortly after I was saved: *God is not against me because of my sin. He is with me against my sin.*

Only because Jesus is with me against my sin can I say to gays everywhere, "God can change your life too if you seek Him honestly and turn yourself over to Him without reservation." Then you can say with me, "*Such were some of us, but now we are washed, sanctified, and justified in the name of the Lord Jesus Christ and in the Spirit of the Lord.*" (See 1 Corinthians 6:11.)

Kevin Linehan is pastor of the Risen Saviour's Christian Fellowship, Reno, Nevada, and director of their ex-gay, transient, and prison correspondence ministries.

Linehan has a Bachelor of Science degree in Communications from the University of Nevada at Reno. He is currently a candidate for the Master of Theology Degree from Toledo Bible School, Tennyson, Indiana.

His writing has appeared in *Gospel Herald, Mennonite Brethren Herald,* and *Forum,* and he is the author of three tracts.

Regarding *Such Were Some of You,* the author says, "I make it very clear that not all homosexuals have the same experiences as I have had nor do I claim to speak for all gays or ex-gay Christians.

"However, the major themes which run through the book are readily discernible in one form or another in most homosexuals' lives, at least those who end up surrendering their lives to Christ.

"I believe that God is not against the gay because of his sin, but rather that He is with the gay against his sin."

If you wish to contact Pastor Linehan simply write to him at: Risen Saviour's Christian Fellowship, P.O. Box 8348, Reno, Nevada 89507 or call the homosexual hotline number, (702) 786-9352. Free tracts and literature regarding homosexuality are available on request.